NINA RAINE

Nina Raine's other plays include *Tiger Country* (Hampstead Theatre, London, 2011 and 2014), *Tribes* (Royal Court, London, 2010/Barrow Street Theatre, New York, 2012) and an adaptation of *The Drunks* by the Durnenkov Brothers (Royal Shakespeare Company, 2009). She was shortlisted for the 2004 Verity Bargate Award and awarded the 2006 Evening Standard and Critics' Circle Awards for Most Promising Playwright for her debut play *Rabbit*. *Tribes* won the Drama Desk Award for outstanding play, the New York Drama Critics' Circle Award for Best Foreign Play and the Off-Broadway Alliance Award for Best New Play. It has also been produced in LA, Chicago, throughout Europe and the rest of the world, having been translated into over ten different languages including Croatian, Estonian, Italian, German, Hebrew, Hungarian, Japanese, Korean, Portuguese, Spanish and Swedish.

Other Titles in this Series

Nina Raine

CONSENT

NICK HERN BOOKS

London

www.nickhernbooks.co.uk

A Nick Hern Book

Consent first published in Great Britain as a paperback original in 2017 by Nick Hern Books Limited, The Glasshouse, 49a Goldhawk Road, London W12 8QP

Consent copyright © 2017 Nina Raine

Nina Raine has asserted her right to be identified as the author of this work

Cover image: Lovers (6) © Jarek Puczel

Designed and typeset by Nick Hern Books, London
Printed and bound in Great Britain by CPI Group (UK) Ltd

A CIP catalogue record for this book is available from the British Library

ISBN 978 1 84842 630 6

MIX
Paper from
responsible sources
FSC
www.fsc.org
FSC® C013604

Consent was first performed as a co-production with Out of Joint in the Dorfman auditorium of the National Theatre, London, on 4 April 2017 (previews from 28 March). The cast, in order of speaking, was as follows:

JAKE	Adam James
KITTY	Anna Maxwell Martin
EDWARD	Ben Chaplin
RACHEL	Priyanga Burford
TIM	Pip Carter
GAYLE/LAURA	Heather Craney
ZARA	Daisy Haggard

Director	Roger Michell
Set Designer	Hildegard Bechtler
Costume Designer	Dinah Collin
Lighting Designer	Rick Fisher
Music	Kate Whitely
Sound Designer	John Leonard
Company Voice Work/ Dialect Coach	Charmian Hoare
Staff Director	Titas Halder

Acknowledgements

This play would not have been possible without the help of
Kathy, Guy, Moses Raine, Craig Raine, Ann Pasternak-Slater,
Lydia Fox, Tamara Oppenheimer, Alex McBride, Tim Owen,
Ramin Gray, Jonathan Levy, Laura Rosefield, Robin Bienenstock,
Jeremy Posnansky, Anthony Morris, Maximilian Hardy,
Will Eaglestone, Ian McEwan, Annalena McAfee, Roger Michell
and Max Stafford-Clark.

Many thanks also to the wonderful actors who performed
readings of the play: Adam James, Pip Carter, Susannah Wise,
Susan Vidler, Tobias Menzies, Mariah Gale, Katherine Tozer,
Michelle Terry, Kate Dickie, Leo Bill, Nikki Amuka-Bird and
Kate Fleetwood.

N.R.

To Kathy and Guy

Characters

JAKE, *mid to late thirties*
KITTY, *mid to late thirties*
EDWARD, *mid to late thirties*
RACHEL, *mid to late thirties*
TIM, *mid to late thirties*
GAYLE, *thirties/forties*
ZARA, *mid to late thirties*
LAURA, *thirties/forties*

Gayle and Laura should be doubled.

This text went to press before the end of rehearsals and so may differ slightly from the play as performed.

ACT ONE

Scene One

A sitting room in a house – high ceilings. A slightly deserted feeling. Some cardboard boxes stand half-opened, an abandoned sofa.

The figure of GAYLE *materialises, dressed in black, at the back of the space. She surveys the room dispassionately.*

Then, she melts away.

And suddenly we are in the midst of a brightly lit, ad-libbed noisy housewarming, among the boxes and sofa. KITTY *is holding a baby.* JAKE *and* EDWARD *stand on either side of her, looking down at the newborn.* RACHEL *stands nearby, drinking wine and watching.* KITTY *offers the baby to* JAKE.

NB Throughout the scene, KITTY *and* EDWARD *touch each other affectionately.*

JAKE *raises his voice above the others.*

JAKE. Oh, yes, *please*!

    The baby is gingerly passed over.

    Aaahh. They're lovely when they're this size. They've got a sort of *spicy* smell, haven't they? What a lot of hair! And – (*Inspecting baby more closely. Sudden respect.*)
    Wow.
    He's got a *massive* head, hasn't he?

KITTY. Yes. When the GP saw him, he said – (*Tones of awe.*) 'Was he *vaginal*?'

JAKE. God. – And was he?

KITTY. *Yes!*

JAKE. Respect.

EDWARD. How's yours?

JAKE. Oh, fantastic. He did a brilliant picture of an apple the other day. I said, Jimmy, that is the most *fantastic* apple, and he said, it's not an apple, Dad, it's a bird, pretending to be an apple.

KITTY. Aah…

RACHEL. He wants a remote-controlled tree for Christmas.

KITTY. *Sweet.* And the little one?

JAKE. Oh, brilliant.

RACHEL. He's crawling.

KITTY (*worried*). Crawling? Really? Already?

RACHEL (*airily*). Oh yes, been crawling for weeks now.

EDWARD. God.

RACHEL (*comfortingly*). – But, he *is* bald. (*To* KITTY.) Oh don't look so *worried*! This is your first! When you have your second, you'll be thinking, '*Please* don't start crawling yet! *Be* a late bloomer, for God's sake!'
– Oh Kitty –

She has noticed that KITTY *is suddenly tearful.*

KITTY.…Sorry… Just… every little thing… you know… *is* a worry… I think it's the lack of sleep, you lose all sense of perspective…

RACHEL. Oh Kitty… of course you do… (*Hugs her.*)

Meanwhile.

JAKE. All right Ed. I've got to ask it. Why didn't you ask me to be godfather?

RACHEL. Jake…

JAKE. I *am* offended. Who else is it going to be? Did you think I wasn't up to it? Is my vagina not big enough?

EDWARD. No. It's not that.

JAKE. So why?

RACHEL. I don't know why you care. (*To the others*.) He said he wouldn't *do* this.

JAKE. 'It's not a difficult question.'

EDWARD. Listen…

JAKE. 'Yes or no will suffice.'

EDWARD. We just decided we weren't going to *have* godparents.

JAKE. Really? Why not?

EDWARD. Too many people to offend.

KITTY. And we don't believe in God.

RACHEL. God? It's all about the presents, isn't it?

EDWARD. Come on, Jake.

JAKE. No, I *am* just a little bit offended, actually, and…

EDWARD. You are an egotist, the loveliest egotist I know, but this is a perfectly understandable feeling, Jake, and it's called –

JAKE. Friendship.

EDWARD. Solipsism. We love you. You know that.

JAKE (*good-naturedly*). Oh, fuck off.

EDWARD. I'm sorry.

JAKE. I forgive you.

EDWARD. Thank you.

    RACHEL *raises her glass*.

RACHEL. To *Leo*.

    They all clink glasses, repeat the toast, drink, etc.

JAKE. And to *Kitty*, for delivering him vaginally.

    They all gravely toast again – 'To Kitty' and 'Vaginally'.

KITTY. Ed wants another one.

RACHEL. What, *already*?

KITTY. I say never again. – Mind you, Ed cried more than I did at the birth.

EDWARD. I found it very upsetting... I still do...

KITTY. You weren't the one in stirrups...

EDWARD. ...Just seeing this person you love and you can't help her... there's absolutely nothing you can do...

Suddenly he can't speak.

JAKE. Oh Ed!

RACHEL. *Both* of you...!

EDWARD *is tearful.*

EDWARD. Sorry, keeps happening to me... like I'm going through the menopause... these hot flushes of emotion...

JAKE *hugs* EDWARD *with one arm, awkwardly, the baby in his other arm.*

KITTY. Yes... Both of us... it was so strange, when the baby came out, when I saw him, it was this weird recognition, 'Oh – it's *you*...'

RACHEL. God, when *our* little man came out, I was like 'Oh. It's my mother-in-law.'

KITTY. Well of course, I've had Ed's mother trying to teach me to *breastfeed*, yanking my nipples, otherwise we've kind of barricaded ourselves in...

EDWARD. The tyranny of people with their champagne, knocking on the door... not *you*, of course...

KITTY. So we're a mess... And *it's* a mess... I'm so sorry...

RACHEL. No, no, it's cool.

JAKE. I love the smell of paint.

EDWARD. We haven't really unpacked yet... fucking estate agent...

KITTY. And we keep *arguing* about how to arrange everything.
The sofas. Facing each other or facing the fireplace –

EDWARD. Well, you want the flow through the room, don't you.

KITTY. So for the moment we've dumped everything where it is.

RACHEL. Great. (*Looking at a lamp in an opened box.*)
Amazing lamp.

KITTY. Look, I found this on eBay –

*She goes and gets an old counterweight and pulley from
a cardboard box.*

We're going to fill it with sand so it balances the weight of
the lamp...

RACHEL (*handling it carefully*). Oh my God. It's a
counterweight.

KITTY (*demonstrating the mechanism*)....Winch it up and
down.

JAKE. Can you...

JAKE is giving the baby to EDWARD. *He winces.*

...*Big*, isn't he, for four weeks? (*Stretches.*) Thanks... Just...
re*align* my back...

EDWARD....So what have you been up to, lately?

JAKE is pouring himself more wine.

JAKE (*wearily*). Me? Oh, I've been raping pensioners.

EDWARD. Charming.

JAKE. Yes. I tie them up, I fuck them, and then I nick their
stuff.

RACHEL. Quite a few of them, apparently.

EDWARD (*to* RACHEL). What about you?

RACHEL. Me? Oh, God. Well, murder.

EDWARD. Oh, I heard about that.

KITTY. Ooh! Murder, who have you murdered?

RACHEL. It's very dull… an old girlfriend, the usual thing.

KITTY. What's the motive?

RACHEL. Sexual, of course. Is there anything that *doesn't* stem from a sexual motive?

She addresses them all.

I mean actually. Really. I'm completely serious. Name me *one thing* that doesn't stem from a sexual motive.

JAKE (*instantly*). Tax.

RACHEL (*wonderingly considers it*). Oh my God. You're right! It's like you've just invented a new element in the Periodic Table.

(*To* EDWARD.) What about you?

EDWARD. Spot of rape too, actually.

RACHEL (*interested*). *Really?* I didn't think you did that sort of thing?

EDWARD (*rocking the baby*). No, well, I don't usually, but Rupert said did I want to, so I thought, why not…

RACHEL. Oh, right…

EDWARD. I raped this woman, Scottish lady, no witnesses – (*Starts putting on Scottish accent.*) she's a bit of a drinker, so am I, her word against mine.

KITTY. Ed's so heartless. He just thinks there's another good accent for me to do. Like the Geordie paedophile.

EDWARD. Oh, he was brilliant value. (*Puts on a Geordie accent in a very high-pitched voice.*) 'I'm telling you, I didn't do it, this will ruin my life, please, you've got to believe me!' (*Reverting to own voice.*) Anyway what's interesting in *this* case is that I'm incredibly promiscuous as well as being a rapist. All these Sharons and Traceys keep coming out of the woodwork. You know, one of the coppers in the case was actually shagging me?

JAKE. *Really?* A bent copper?

EDWARD. Yeah. Lots of juicy circumstantial evidence. Apparently she's got a raised mole near her vagina. *And* I've been shagging a schoolgirl.

RACHEL. Ooh, not good.

EDWARD. No. In fact, as far as I can work out, I was shagging everyone within shagging distance.

JAKE. Oh dear.

EDWARD. Yep. So I was shagging –

He counts them off on his fingers.

The Scottish lady, the corrupt copper, the schoolgirl, and that's just the ones we know about. I'm going to exclude it, it's all prejudicial.

KITTY. Sounds it. (*Mildly curious, she ruffles his hair.*) What happened with the schoolgirl?

EDWARD. Going by the text messages, a lot. She's filthy. (*Puts on an Essex accent.*) 'I'm going to suck your cock and wank you off and lick your balls…'

KITTY *takes the baby from him, heads offstage – as she goes:*

KITTY. All at the same time?

EDWARD. Well of course it's all part of the evidence. She wrote in one text – (*Puts on a lascivious voice.*) '…And then I've got my *Spanish oral…* ' I thought, 'Wow. What the hell's a *Spanish* oral? I'm living a very sheltered life.' – She was talking about her GCSEs.

JAKE. God. I often think how dreadful it would be if someone went through *my* text messages.

RACHEL. Yes, it's unfair really, it's so easy to make people look stupid.

JAKE. Mmm.

EDWARD (*puts on barristerial tone*). 'Oh it was a *joke*, was it? I see. Not a very *funny* joke, was it?'

KITTY *comes back in.*

KITTY. Basically, Ed, you *tease* people for a living.

EDWARD (*to* RACHEL). So do you think you've got a run?

RACHEL. Dunno, really. What about you?

EDWARD. Erm… (*Decisively.*) No. (*Croons to the baby.*) 'No, I don't think we *do* have a case, do we… nooo.' Which is a shame.

Tim's prosecuting, though, which is a laugh.

RACHEL. Oh Tim! Is he still single?

EDWARD. Eternally.

RACHEL. Poor Tim.

KITTY. He's so eligible.

JAKE. But he smells.

KITTY. No he doesn't.

EDWARD. Yes, he does. We had to have a word with him.

RACHEL. How did he respond to the allegation?

JAKE. Started wearing Lynx.

KITTY (*from off*). Shut up. We must find him someone. He wants *kids*.

EDWARD. But should those genes be passed *on*?

JAKE (*thoughtfully*). *I* once shagged a girl with a mole on her vagina.

EDWARD (*brightening*). Did you? Really?

JAKE. Gave me quite a fright.

EDWARD. Where was it?

JAKE *makes an upside-down V with his fingers, a makeshift vagina, points to the left finger.*

JAKE. Right here.

EDWARD. Interesting. Did you spend ages on it?

RACHEL*, who has been checking her phone, drains her drink.*

RACHEL. Guys, we're going to have to head.

JAKE. Already?

RACHEL. It's been so lovely, but you're exhausted, and we should get back. (*To* JAKE.) He's not been sleeping well.

KITTY. Oh, really?

RACHEL. Yeah.

They start to gather jackets, etc.

JAKE. She's lying. She just wants to get back to her case, fucking workaholic.

RACHEL. That's right. You know we sit there in bed, the two of us side by side, with our marker pens, and I think – (*Mock bliss.*) 'Does it get better than this?'

JAKE. No, it's true, we should go. Jimmy told Rachel he's been having nightmares.

RACHEL. Except, he said 'You had nightmare.'

JAKE. He doesn't say 'I' and 'Me' yet.

KITTY. Really?

RACHEL. It's so sweet.

EDWARD. What does he say?

RACHEL. He says 'You'.

JAKE. Because that's what everyone else calls him. He calls himself 'You'. 'You want more raisins.'

KITTY. Wow.

RACHEL. It's actually completely logical.

JAKE. He'll get the hang in the end.

RACHEL. It's so lovely. He's just this little person, just beginning to learn about everything. Trying to explain the way he feels.

They all kiss goodbye.

KITTY. That was lovely.

EDWARD. It was. See you soon.

RACHEL. You're both going to be *fine*. See you soon.

KITTY. Promise.

RACHEL. I promise.

JAKE. See you soon.

EDWARD and KITTY see them out. Noise of doors opening, closing, 'Goodbyes' from off. EDWARD comes back in, starts to clear wine glasses, etc. KITTY follows, ditto. The tone between EDWARD and KITTY alone is quite different.

KITTY. Do you think they're all right?

EDWARD. What?

KITTY. Do you think they're okay?

EDWARD. Yes. Why?

Beat.

KITTY. I don't know…

You know. I thought she seemed…

Beat.

He kept bringing up sex. Didn't you think?

EDWARD. We all kept bringing up sex.

Beat. KITTY goes off, comes back on again with a bundled-up white tablecloth.

KITTY. Help me fold.

They start to fold the tablecloth together, carefully matching up the edges.

What about when they were talking about texts.

EDWARD. It was *me* who was talking about texts.

KITTY. No, *she* said 'It's so easy to make people look stupid.' About reading people's texts.

I thought there was an edge to it.

EDWARD. God, no.

Beat. The tablecloth is folded into a small square. They look at each other.

I think they're absolutely fine.

He kisses her.

Scene Two

GAYLE *sits nervously waiting, cheaply but smartly dressed.* TIM *comes up in a hurry, checking his phone as he comes. He is dressed in a suit with a collarless white shirt.* GAYLE *speaks in a strong Scottish accent.*

TIM. Hi, I'm sorry, I don't know where the Witness Services has disappeared to again, I think she went to get a coffee, rather than hang about I just wanted to introduce myself, and explain, there's a legal argument happening at the moment, hence the delay, plus they still haven't got the wifi working in the court, but once the jury have been sworn in, very soon after that, we will be good to go. I'm sorry as I know you may be feeling nervous –

GAYLE. Who are you?

TIM. Oh sorry! I'm the prosecuting barrister, sorry don't have my wig on yet. Erm so yes, it's me that asks you some questions first about what happened and then the defence will ask you some questions about what happened, cross-examine you and that part will be a bit like going to the dentist, not much fun I'm afraid –

GAYLE. Are you the one on my side then?

TIM. Erm that's a good question, that's a good question. I'm here to represent what you said happened, and present the case against Mr Taylor so –

GAYLE. But are you my lawyer?

TIM. …Strictly speaking I'm not your lawyer, no.

GAYLE. Who are you then?

TIM. I'm – I'm the lawyer for the crown, the crown's case.

GAYLE. But I'm the one it happened to.

TIM. I know, I know it did.

GAYLE. So who's my lawyer?

TIM. You don't actually have a lawyer.

GAYLE. But it happened to me.

TIM. I know, I know it did but technically you're a witness, the case is against Mr Taylor.

GAYLE. Does he get a lawyer?

TIM. Yes and in fact that brings me to my next point, it's now part of my job to give you some information, and I must tell you the defence case in this case is that you consented.

GAYLE. I what?

TIM. You consented to sex with Mr Taylor.

GAYLE. I did what?

TIM. You consented to sex with Mr Taylor, you invited him to stay the night with you –

GAYLE. God Almighty! He was drinking with Teddy, I went to bed, I was finished, I was in bits, the day of my little sister's funeral and then at 3 a.m. I wake up with him on top of me –

TIM. I'm sorry I should have made this clear, this can't be the start of a conversation between us, I simply have to give you that information, I can't give you advice on how to –

GAYLE. He's on top of me and he's trying to take my pyjama bottoms off of me, I push him like this with my arm I said what in God's name d'you think you're doing, he grabs my top and the whole pocket rips –

TIM. Look, it's really unfortunate but I mustn't get into a discussion with you about it now. You need to tell the court what happened in your own words, and I will do my very best to help you with my questions. I understand it's a nerve-racking experience but if you want a break the court will break, you just pause and you take your time, you'll be behind a screen –

GAYLE. I don't want a screen.

Beat.

TIM. Okay. Okay.

Beat.

It's much easier if you don't have your attacker looking at you –

GAYLE. I will look at him and say what he did, I can't believe what he did on the day of my sister's funeral – !

TIM. You need to say all this in court.

GAYLE. But I need to tell you –

TIM. No. Not to me, it's actually quite important you don't say it to me, not now.

GAYLE. Why?

TIM. Because then I would be helping you practise which isn't allowed, you need to say all this in court. What you should do *now* is take a moment to read your statement that you made to the police – have you read your statement?

GAYLE. I know what happened! He pulled my pyjama bottoms down and he was pushing me down –

TIM. Right well it's good you have the events fresh in your memory, but please read your statement because the lawyers will be relying on it and its accuracy –

GAYLE. But there are things I didn't say in my statement.

Beat.

TIM. Okay okay okay now hold on a minute. This is very important.

GAYLE. That's why I need to tell you –

TIM. There are things you didn't say in your statement?

GAYLE. Yes.

TIM. Okay. *If* there are things you didn't say in your statement for *whatever* reason, whether you forgot or whether there was another reason –

GAYLE. I was frightened of him.

Beat.

TIM. That's a good reason, that's a good reason. But you *cannot* tell me things you haven't said in your statement. Not to me, not now. Because you'll make me a witness. And then I won't be able to prosecute the case.

GAYLE. I was crying, he couldn't get it in, he was pushing forwards and backwards. He was hurting me.

TIM. Stop. Okay. Let me get the Officer in the Case.

GAYLE. He went down and he licked me. He said you like a man doing this, this is what you like. I was saying stop. He said, it's what you like, you like a man doing this.

He raped me.

They look at each other. TIM *leaves.*

Scene Three

KITTY, EDWARD, JAKE, TIM *and* ZARA *are all in the*
sitting room drinking, all laughing. EDWARD *is rolling a joint.*
TIM *is dry and lugubrious.* ZARA *is attractive. The boxes are*
gone. The Moses basket is still there but the furniture is
arranged differently, a bit more inhabited. Otherwise the setting
is as it was before. ZARA *struggles to make herself heard.*

ZARA. No I *mean* it! It's *so* lovely!

JAKE. Again, with conviction.

ZARA. I *mean* it!

> EDWARD *is approaching them with a wine bottle and a*
> *child's bottle in the other hand.*

EDWARD. Can I fill you up?

ZARA. Oh God… I am tempted…

EDWARD. She says no but she means yes.

ZARA. I shouldn't, I'm hungover.

> JAKE *grabs the wine bottle. On the babycom, the baby starts*
> *to grizzle.*

JAKE (*pouring*). Oh, we're all *hungover.*

KITTY. This is the trouble. I've been feeding him whenever he
cries so he feeds to sleep.

JAKE. So what. I feed to sleep.

TIM. I *drink* to sleep.

ZARA. I <u>cry</u> to sleep.

> KITTY *has taken the baby's bottle off* EDWARD *and gone*
> *out to listen better.*

– Honestly. It's *so* lovely here.

EDWARD. Yeah. We've only been broken in to once.

> *He lights the joint.* KITTY *shouts from off.*

KITTY. Come on, Ed, he didn't even get into the house. We saw a man in the garden.

EDWARD. About eleven o'clock at night.
I rang the police.

KITTY *comes back in.*

KITTY. Unfortunately Ed was stoned at the time.

EDWARD. They asked me what the intruder looked like and all I could say was – (*Dazed, stoned voice.*) 'He had… a *face*…' Kitty was worried their Alsatians would smell my hash. End of my legal career.

KITTY. So in the end we told them not to come round.

But yes, it *is* lovely.

EDWARD *offers the joint to* TIM.

TIM (*thoughtfully*). Mm… I'd smoke it more often but I get these terrible…

EDWARD. Flashbacks?

TIM. Sore throats. (*To* ZARA.) So why are you hungover?

ZARA. I was out drinking after rehearsals.

KITTY (*to* ZARA). Ooh!! – How *is* it?!

JAKE. How's the director?

EDWARD. Is she mad?

ZARA (*carefully*). No. She's very enthusiastic, very free, very –

JAKE. Mad.

KITTY. What's the play like?

ZARA. Well, you know. It's Greek.

EDWARD *is checking his phone.*

EDWARD. Oh, the gods always appear.

KITTY. I get confused when they start *repenting* all over the place.

EDWARD. They're just fundamentally unpleasant people, aren't they?

TIM. The men are shits and the women are insufferable because they're so holier-than-thou. Right?

ZARA. Well, *I'm* not holier-than-thou –

JAKE. Seriously. Is it *fun*? Is it a fun night out?

ZARA. – No.

KITTY. It'll be great! Don't listen to them.

ZARA. …No, you're right, it *is* great, you know, before you mistreat your women, remember what they're capable of –

JAKE. / Right.

ZARA. / – what if one of them takes revenge? What if one of them was a goddess? What then?

EDWARD. You know there's a Medea Complex in law?

ZARA. Really?

EDWARD. Premeditated calculation rather than insanity.

ZARA. Can't you calculatingly premeditate and *be* insane?

KITTY. What's the concept?

ZARA. Well… the director *is* great… very bold…

JAKE. Ye-es…

ZARA. And she wants us to do it in accents.

TIM. Accents?

ZARA. First it was Scottish. Then it was Northern Irish. That's okay: I think of a person I know and – (*Puts on Northern Irish accent.*) make my face like theirs. Y'know. (*Continuing in Northern Irish accent.*) Should I stop noi? Or can I carry oin? (*Back to normal voice.*) But I'm just hoping to God it's not going to end up Yorkshire. My Yorkshire is terrible.

EDWARD. Yorkshire? (*Yorkshire accent.*) 'Zeus'?

ZARA. Or *Cornish* – Jesus.

KITTY. That's the thing about high concept, it's like Pringles – quite *moreish*.

JAKE. But if *anyone* can be RP, surely the gods can.

ZARA. I'm not playing a god, I'm playing *her* and my Yorkshire is absolutely appalling.

TIM. What, sort of, 'Ee bah gum, pet, night, black night, nurse of golden stars, night in which I go to fetch t'waters of t'river's streams and send forth groans for my father into the vast sky.'

KITTY (*to* ZARA). Tim read Classics at uni.

TIM. And my dad's a Yorkshireman.

ZARA. – Wow! How come you –

TIM. Became a barrister? I don't know. Deeply crap idea.

ZARA. *Fantastic!* So tell them. It *is* great, isn't it.

TIM. Oh yeah. It's your classic Greek play.

EDWARD. Which is?

TIM. Two opposing characters holding two relative but mutually destructive truths. (*The wine*.) Can I have a bit more of that?

EDWARD. Meaning?

TIM. Wine.

ZARA. Tragedy. That's tragedy.

KITTY. No, it's two people thinking they're right.

EDWARD. No no no, the *mainstay* of Greek plays is priggish characters taking the moral high-ground, *I* could have told you that.

TIM. Fuck that, the golden rule for any Greek play is, an unbonked woman goes bonkers.

ZARA. Oh well, that's true for me, *definitely*! I only murder my children because I know it's what'll hurt Jason most, because sadism's really a twisted empathy, isn't it, and...

Beat.

Ooh, everyone's quiet and listening to me now.

JAKE (*brightly*). Don't worry.
It's because we're bored.

ZARA. Well, you'll be interested to hear, Jason's going to be nude for the final scene.

EDWARD. Bloody hell. Let's all have a drink.

He fills them all up.

I become even nicer when I'm drunk.

He looks at the label.

Zara, you shame us. This is by far the most expensive bottle.

ZARA. I've got disposable income, I rent in Zone 4.

KITTY. You look tired, Tim. How's life?

TIM (*to* ZARA). I'm just in the process of moving house. (*Generally.*) I feel like a squatter. Just got a mattress there. Actually, I think it's haunted.

JAKE. Seriously?

ZARA. How?

TIM. I keep waking up in the middle of the night. And it's always at exactly 2.59 a.m. Every night, without fail. I know it is, because I've got a digital display and I thought, is this because I should be watching the Ashes in Australia? England *do* do better when I'm watching... But then, the other night, I pulled this girl –

JAKE. Whoa, now *that's* a story! Bloody hell, Tim, you kept that quiet! What girl? When?

TIM. It's no big deal.

JAKE. Yes, it is! (*To* ZARA.) This man's a workaholic, he hasn't had intercourse to my knowledge for the last three years –

TIM. Thanks, Jake, for that, anyway –

JAKE. Who is she?

KITTY. Stop interrupting, I want to hear about the fucking ghost!

TIM. She stayed the night, and at 2.59, I woke up, as usual, and the fucking kettle flew across the room.

Beat.

EDWARD. Flew across the room, what do you mean?

TIM. I mean, it went bash! Across the room and into the opposite wall like someone had picked it up and thrown it.

Beat.

JAKE. Fucking hell.

Beat.

What did the girl say?

TIM. She was dead to the world. We'd drunk a *lot*.

EDWARD (*slyly*). Of course.

TIM. I just got out of bed, picked it up and put it back.

Beat.

ZARA. So what are you going to do?

TIM. I called a psychic.

JAKE. A *psychic*?

EDWARD. Next he'll be telling us he believes in God.

KITTY. Where did you get hold of a psychic?

TIM. Google. One consultation over the phone, sixty quid. She also did home visits, but that was a hundred and sixty quid, which seemed a bit much, to me.

EDWARD (*shrugging*). That's what it costs, nowadays…

TIM. Anyway, she asked me some questions about myself, and I asked her some questions.

KITTY. What did you ask her?

EDWARD. 'Who am I?'

ZARA. Sounds like therapy. I should do it, I've got loads of questions. 'Is this the man I'm going to marry?'

TIM. And she said a couple of things that were surprisingly insightful, and a lot of things that were pretty irrelevant.

ZARA. *Just* like therapy.

TIM. It seemed to work because there hasn't been a peep out of her since.

JAKE. The ghost or the girl?

TIM. Oh, fuck off.

TIM *rouses himself.*

I'd better go. (*To* ZARA.) This case.

KITTY. Oh, Tim, *really*?

TIM. Sorry.

EDWARD. Come on, Tim, I'm cross-ex*ami*ning tomorrow. You just sit there with a bland look on your face.

TIM. My complainant can be amazingly incoherent in the dock. (*Meaningfully.*) Especially when she's deliberately being wound up.

EDWARD. I cannot wait to hear her victim's *impact* statement.

TIM. I need to win for that to happen, mate.

EDWARD. Victims shouldn't have a role in punishment, anyway.

KITTY. Why not?

EDWARD. Because then it becomes about *vengeance*. Obviously.

KITTY. What's wrong with a bit of vengeance?

ZARA. Apparently people who forgive unconditionally live longer.

EDWARD. Well there's a good selfish reason to do it.

TIM (*to* JAKE). We're midway through some filth.

EDWARD (*to* JAKE). We've got the big red-faced shouting Welsh judge. Thingy.

TIM is getting up, stretching, looking around for his jumper, etc.

JAKE. Oh, *him*. He's an absolute cunt.

KITTY. Oh! I thought he was warm and bubbly.

TIM. Yes, a warm bubbly cunt.

JAKE. I wish he would *die*. Could we not arrange for pancreatic cancer through the post?

TIM. I'll ask the gods.

KITTY. Which reminds me, Zara's got a big audition for a legal drama. You must help her with her research.

TIM. Of course, of course.

ZARA. Not now. Anyway.

TIM. It was lovely to meet you at last.

ZARA. Lovely.

They gingerly kiss.

JAKE. Give old Welshbag a kiss from me.

TIM. Will do. Bye, folks.

KITTY. I'll see you out.

He goes. KITTY goes out after him. We hear their voices from off. JAKE, ZARA and EDWARD wait in silence, JAKE and EDWARD looking at ZARA. ZARA avoids their eyes, drinks wine.

Noise of the front door opening and closing. KITTY *comes back in. Looks at them all. She turns to* ZARA.

Well?

ZARA. No. I'm really sorry.

In unison.

KITTY. / Really? Why??

EDWARD. / I told you so!

JAKE. / I thought you wouldn't.

KITTY.…What a shame…

ZARA.…But you know how it *is*…

KITTY. I just thought, you know…

JAKE (*with finality*). I could have told you so.

ZARA. You knew as well? God, how embarrassing!

KITTY. But *why*?

ZARA. Well, he's *gay*, isn't he?

EDWARD. Not gay. Might look gay. But not gay.

ZARA. Oh, okay. *Fey?*

KITTY. He wants *kids*…

ZARA. So do *I*, but how many ways can I say it –

JAKE. You can't. It's impossible to communicate the pheremonal semiology of sexual attraction –

ZARA. – I just don't fancy him.

EDWARD. There you go. (*To* ZARA.) Well, why should you fancy him. I don't fancy him. (*To* KITTY.) Do you fancy him? – Because he's always fancied *you*.

KITTY. Rubbish.

EDWARD. He drools over you.

KITTY. He does not *drool* over me.

EDWARD. No, you're absolutely right, Zara. I realised I was staring at him trying to work out what animal he reminded me of.

ZARA. Otter?

EDWARD. Otter's too glamorous. Hamster?

ZARA. He was just a bit, *victim*-y… and his *aftershave*…

KITTY. Oh, that's not *fair*…

JAKE. Look, we can't advocate for the guy. Leave Zara to find her own men. She looks perfectly capable to me.

ZARA. No, no… many hands make light work… Maybe I should go for a *younger* man… There are plenty of young fathers nowadays…

EDWARD. Most of them in prison, but…

ZARA *starts to gather herself to go.*

ZARA. Yeah, yeah, but I've got to hurry up and have children, at *some* point in the future, as insurance, you know, to look after me when I'm old, and you do start to wonder, what is *wrong* with me, when you look at some of the *losers* and *lunatics* who have managed to have kids – not you lot, obviously – you end up thinking, like *Lear*, 'Why should a dog, a rat, a horse have life, and *thou* no breath at all?'

EDWARD. Yes… I felt like that when I kept failing my *driving* test… how come all those *other* morons managed it…

ZARA (*generally*). Honestly, how *did* you lot manage it?

JAKE. Theirs was an arranged marriage, they grew to love each other.

ZARA. The child brought them together.

KITTY *and* EDWARD *laugh.*

JAKE. They're laughing on the outside, crying on the inside.

ZARA *gets her bag.*

ZARA. I don't want to go, because –

EDWARD. You'll bump into him, outside.

ZARA. – you'll slag *me* off instead.

KITTY. Zara, for God's sake, will you let me pay for a cab?

EDWARD. Zone 4? We couldn't possibly afford it.

EDWARD and KITTY *start to exit with* ZARA *to see her out.*

KITTY. We'll come and see you in the play.

ZARA. Oh yes. It is *such* a great part.

We hear their voices from off.

Why don't people write parts like that for *women* any more? Parts where you get to scream and *rage*? Parts like *Lear*?

KITTY (*following them off*). Because if *Lear* was a woman everyone would say 'It's her hormones.'

JAKE remains, alone. He rubs his face and we see the gaiety drain away from him. Sound of the door closing after some murmured conversation. EDWARD *and* KITTY *come back in. There is a different atmosphere.* EDWARD *and* KITTY *look intently at* JAKE, *who stretches self-consciously and elaborately. A long pause.*

EDWARD. So. What's going on?

JAKE. What?

EDWARD. You look *terrible*.

JAKE. Thanks.

Pause.

KITTY. What happened?

JAKE. What do you mean, what happened?

EDWARD and KITTY *look at each other.*

KITTY. When I rang Rachel she sounded really odd.

EDWARD. Come on, Jakey.

Pause.

JAKE. She's chucked me out.

KITTY. *Why?*

Pause.

JAKE. Oh, God… All right then.

She's got some mad idea I've been having an affair.

Affairs.

Beat.

Well don't all rush to contradict…

EDWARD. No, no, obviously, but…

JAKE. Look, it's all a complete nonsense. She'll calm down. I'm really not worried.

KITTY. When did she chuck you out?

JAKE. Monday. I'm staying with my brother. In Putney. Which is a whole other nightmare, but anyway…

Beat. He looks at them.

Don't look so *worried*! It's a storm in a teacup. She'll calm down, realise she's being crazy and we'll be back to how we were. Endlessly sniping, like any other healthy marriage.

I promise.

EDWARD. Christ, Jake, I'm so sorry.

KITTY. What made her think…?

JAKE. A text.

Ridiculous. It was a joke.

In unison.

EDWARD. / Who to?

KITTY. / From?

JAKE *sighs heavily.*

JAKE. That pupil, you know, the one with the glasses.

EDWARD. Jemima?

JAKE. No, not Jemima.

EDWARD. Oh, Martha.

JAKE. No! *Laura.* We were arsing around. Rachel for some reason got hold of my phone and read them all. God knows how she guessed my PIN… (*Accusingly.*) she's got a terribly *secretive* streak, Rachel… Fucking iPhone… conversations go *right* back to the beginning… who the hell thought *that* was a good idea?

EDWARD *and* KITTY *look at him.*

I suppose out of context it did look a bit…

But there was nothing going *on*!

And now it's cast doubt on… you know, every time I've been out playing tennis with *you*, or having a con with a *client* or… she's convinced it goes back years and I've just been shagging one woman after another.

Beat.

EDWARD. So it wasn't –

JAKE. What?

EDWARD. You know. Anything to do with.

JAKE. What?

EDWARD. The Hannah Thing.

JAKE. God, no!

No, no no.
She doesn't know about *Hannah*. For Christ's sake, don't tell her about *that*. That would be a disaster.

EDWARD. Well, you were completely indiscreet about it.

JAKE. Oh, Lordy.

That's because I thought it was all a bit of a joke.

That's the *problem*. I mean I love a bit of 'anger' as much as the next guy, but I just can't take it *seriously*. All this drama and shouting at three in the morning. She's particularly bad on red wine, I've noticed.

Rachel said I was just like a typical human-rights barrister.

KITTY. How?

JAKE. Shallow.

I can't bear this attitude, you know, 'My feelings have more *vitamins* than yours.' I am... basically... being *bullied*. And I'm... having to behave quite differently to how I normally would.

KITTY. Not answer back?

JAKE. Yep.

EDWARD. What about Jimmy?

JAKE. It's horrible. We've told him I'm away on a case. I had to say goodnight to him over the phone last night.

KITTY. How was it?

JAKE. A very brief exchange of information. I asked questions, he gave me short polite answers. 'Yes, I've been a good boy. No, I'm going to watch a film about a monkey now.' I felt like the president of a third-world country getting a courtesy call from the White House.

Pause.

What if she takes the kids away from me?

KITTY. She won't.

EDWARD. She wouldn't.

JAKE. She might.

Pause.

I *bet* she's been up to stuff as well. I bet you.
How could she not have?

KITTY. *Jake…*

> *Pause.*

JAKE. Look, it's going to be okay.

> She'll forgive me. I know she will.

> KITTY *and* EDWARD *look at him.*

Scene Four

EDWARD *faces* GAYLE *in the witness box. He has his wig on. There is a subtle pugnacity to his manner.*

EDWARD. You went to bed, didn't you.

GAYLE. Yes.

EDWARD. It was 3 a.m., wasn't it.

GAYLE. 3, 4 a.m.

> EDWARD *looks at his notes.*

EDWARD. You'd been drinking…

GAYLE. Pernod and lemonade.

EDWARD. By my reckoning it was along the lines of ten. Ten or eleven Pernod and lemonade by then, wasn't it?

GAYLE. I don't know. I dinnae remember. It was the day of my sister's funeral, my little sister had just died.

EDWARD. And your brother, Teddy? How much had he had?

GAYLE. I don't know. You dinnae count what people drink.

EDWARD. 'You don't count what people drink.' Hm.

> *Pause.*

Did you take a drink to bed with you?

GAYLE.…I dinnae remember.

Pause.

EDWARD. Were you drunk?

GAYLE. I was upset.

Beat.

EDWARD. Did you invite Mr Taylor to join you in your bed?

GAYLE (*incredulously*). Did I…?

EDWARD. It's a simple question, yes or no will suffice. Did you invite Mr Taylor to join you in your bed?

GAYLE. Not if I were in it, God Amighty!! No!

She laughs angrily.

EDWARD. 'No.'
(*Thoughtfully.*) Ye-es.
'No.'
I see.

A pause. EDWARD *leafs through his notes again.*

In your statement you say that you received a phone call at ten o' clock the next morning from your brother, Teddy, isn't that right.

GAYLE. Aye.

EDWARD. Asking how you were. You said to the officer in your statement. (*Speaks without any attempt at any naturalism but maintaining his crisp RP.*) 'I picked up the phone and I said all right Teddy I cannee speak now I'll phone you back, that's what I said I'll phone you back and then I did I phoned him back that's what I did see.'

GAYLE (*under her breath*). (…Not how I said it…)

EDWARD. That's *correct*, isn't it.

GAYLE.…Yeah.

EDWARD. And you're clear, aren't you, that you didn't mention *anything* to Teddy about what had happened with Mr Taylor at that time?

GAYLE. He was still there.

EDWARD. Who was still there?

GAYLE. He – Mr Taylor was still there.

EDWARD (*putting on a surprised tone*). In your apartment?

GAYLE. Because he hadne left.

EDWARD (*ditto*). Because he hadn't *left*! I see.

Beat.

GAYLE. I came out of my bedroom and I saw him there flat-out on the sofa. I was honestly so shocked to see him still there, / I –

EDWARD. / So after you had had sex, the night before, he stayed –

GAYLE. We didne have sex. He raped me. He left the room after he raped me and I lay there. I didne know what to do.

EDWARD. Did you fall asleep?

GAYLE (*incredulously*). Did I fall *asleep*? I'd just been raped!

Beat.

EDWARD. You didn't call the police?

GAYLE. Because I was scared of him, I was scared of what he might do if I got up, my phone was out there charging in the sitting room, I didne know if he'd left or no.

Beat.

EDWARD. Were you still drunk, would you say?

GAYLE. I was *upset*. I was crying. I was shaking.

Pause. EDWARD *looks at his notes.*

EDWARD. So you accept that you lay there all night, you didn't get up?

GAYLE. Yeh.

EDWARD. And the next morning, you did get up –

GAYLE. / Aye.

EDWARD. / – and you came into the sitting room, and saw Mr Taylor there?

GAYLE. Aye, I saw him there and he woke up, he jumped up, he was looking around for his shoes, he was barefoot I remember because he said something about my underfloor heating.

EDWARD. So you chatted about your underfloor heating?

GAYLE. No! I told you, I was scared of him! Then Teddy called on my mobile, I said I'd call him back, and that was it, Patrick left he was out of there. As soon as he left I called Teddy back, I telt him what had happened, he came straight roond –

EDWARD. Yes, I have his account here.

He says he came round and you talked about what had happened –

GAYLE. Aye, Teddy was so shocked that he could have done a thing like that, he couldne believe what he done on the day of my sister's funeral – !

EDWARD. – And Teddy says he poured himself a drink.

Beat.

What time was this?

GAYLE. …Eleven.

EDWARD. In the morning?

GAYLE. Yes.

Pause.

EDWARD. And Teddy says he poured you a – .

GAYLE. Yes he poured me a drink.

EDWARD. And were you drinking –

GAYLE. Pernod!

EDWARD.…With lemonade?

GAYLE. Yeh! Lemonade!

EDWARD. Were you –

GAYLE. I was upset!

EDWARD. Were you drunk?

GAYLE. Of course I was drunk! Of course I was drunk!!

> EDWARD *looks at his notes. Pause.*

EDWARD. *Then* Mr Taylor sent you a text message.

> GAYLE *just looks at him.*

The text message said, 'Thanks for last night. Hope you're feeling okay.'

And you texted back. You texted back…

He reads from his notes

'*Yeah*
I'm
fine.'

Is that correct?

Long pause.

GAYLE. Yes.

Pause.

EDWARD. *Earlier* that week you had been to see your psychotherapist.

> GAYLE *just looks at him warily.* EDWARD *looks at his notes.*

The jury have heard evidence from your psychotherapist who said, 'After I saw Gayle I wrote up the notes. I wrote that she was her usual self.' I asked 'By "usual self" what do you mean?' Your psychotherapist replied 'Being quite sad and fed up about her life.'

Would you say that's a fair description of yourself?

GAYLE.…I don't know.

EDWARD. You don't know?

GAYLE. I cannae describe meself.

Pause.

EDWARD. Are you paranoid?

GAYLE. What do you mean?

EDWARD. I'd like to ask –

GAYLE. What do you mean by paranoid?

EDWARD. – whether you ever feel you imagine things?

GAYLE. I honestly don't believe this…

EDWARD. Are you familiar with the term, 'hypervigilance'? Do you think it would be fair to say –

GAYLE. I honestly don't believe this, I honestly don't believe the *stuff* you're coming out with! You're trying to make out I'm some *mad* person –

EDWARD. I'm not trying to do anything except ask you some questions –

GAYLE. You're saying I'm *mad* –

EDWARD. I have no wish to quarrel with you -

GAYLE. It happened!

It *happened*, folks.

She turns out and looks at us.

He raped me on the day of my little sister's funeral. He came into my bedroom in the middle of the night and raped me. And I will look at him, there, and say it.

Scene Five

JAKE *sits in* EDWARD *and* KITTY*'s house.* JAKE *has been crying and looks like a wreck.* KITTY *and* EDWARD *are at a loss. He has obviously caught them mid-supper: there is cheese and wine out but* JAKE *is in his coat.*

KITTY. Breathe. Take a breath.

EDWARD. How did it happen. Tell us how it happened.

A pause while JAKE *struggles with heaving sobs.*

JAKE. Oh, *God…* I can't *breathe…*

KITTY *finds a Kleenex, gives it to him. He blows his nose.*

…I've got to *smoke…*

He is already getting out cigarettes.

EDWARD. Of course, of course.

JAKE *lights the cigarette.*

JAKE. I can't believe it…

KITTY. Breathe in…

JAKE. I *am* fucking breathing in, I'm smoking…

He cries a little.

…She won't *listen* to me. It's no use apologising because she doesn't believe me. She doesn't think I *am* sorry. I can't communicate with her. She's locked in *herself*, she's made up her mind…

KITTY. Jake, Jake, stop panicking and – inhale –

EDWARD. What did she say?

JAKE. She wouldn't make eye contact…

KITTY. But what did she *say*?

JAKE *takes a deep breath.*

JAKE. She wants to…

He starts to cry again.

Looking back –
I look back at myself and I don't know who the person was who did those things!

She wants a divorce.

He cries for a beat. KITTY *and* EDWARD *are shocked.*

EDWARD. Go back to the beginning.

KITTY. Yes, the beginning.

JAKE *takes a deep breath.*

JAKE. She'd given him a bath – got Jimmy and the little one to bed. And… I came from the Temple. She cancelled and then she uncancelled at the last minute so… Um, I haven't seen her for about… the last time was…

KITTY. A week?

JAKE. The point is, she kept on rescheduling…

EDWARD. The / weekend?

JAKE. / I don't *know*! It's a blur… The house, um, she's changed er, moved the sofa around, swapped it around to face the windows…

…I've lost my…

KITTY. She got them to bed…

JAKE. That's right, I had a drink, she had a drink, we were both drinking…

EDWARD. What were you drinking…

JAKE. Um, we were standing in the kitchen, she was by the washing machine…

…She says it's over, she can't forgive me. She says… She wants me out of the house, she wants the kids.

We were drinking a bottle of red.

He starts to cry again. During his speech RACHEL *has entered and takes a seat on the opposite side of the stage.*

The staging should arrange RACHEL *apart from* JAKE –
they are not in the same 'scene'.

RACHEL. White. He'd bought a bottle of white. Like that
would make it better.

Jimmy and the little one were upstairs in bed. Masha had
got them to bed, read them a story. I said *if* he cancelled it
would be a week till I could see him, and the *last* time we
saw each other was Thursday, eight days ago. So he came
straight round.

JAKE....If she takes the kids away from me... I'll fucking...
I'm not going to be one of those men... I'll... fucking...

He breaks down.

KITTY (*to both*). Can't you *talk* to each other?

RACHEL/JAKE (*in unison*) We have.

She drinks wine, brooding. JAKE *is suddenly childlike.*
He dries his eyes.

JAKE. What's going to happen to me?

RACHEL (*lost*). What happened to us?

Beat. EDWARD *and* KITTY *turn to* JAKE.

EDWARD. Can you –

JAKE. I can't remember the exact way she said it... She said
something about, about taking me to court. But I can't tell
you *why*. I don't understand it. As far as I can see, *I* want
something from *her*.

He cries again.

Jimmy's finally got the hang of calling himself 'I'.

You know what he says for 'I don't remember?' – 'I didn't see
me doing that.' Did you play on the swings yesterday? He
thinks and he goes, 'Um... no... I didn't see me doing that.'

RACHEL. He says he looks back to the person he was when he
married me and he doesn't know who that is.
He doesn't seem to realise the *damage*!

KITTY. You're sure you're not being paranoid?

RACHEL. He gave me an STD.
Pubic lice.

They turn to JAKE.

JAKE. I thought she knew what was going on! I was so *obvious* about it!

KITTY.... *What* did you think she knew?

JAKE. *Everything...*
You have this fantasy that someone loves you for yourself...
You and all your flaws...
I know it sounds naive... But – ... Someone who's going to let you *be* who you *are*.

KITTY.... That's your *mother*.

JAKE. I was lying to myself that she *knew*, that she knew and she *accepted* it.

She was lying to herself that nothing was going on.

RACHEL *swigs her wine*.

RACHEL. Okay. For example. He always leaves his receipts in his pockets and they cover everything with white fluff. So I empty them out when I do the *cunting* laundry. 'One Prawn Sandwich, Paddington M&S.' But he hates prawns. He said it was for a client. I looked in the bathroom cabinet. He'd taken hair gel. But why do you need hair gel when you're in Hove, in court, wearing a *wig* all day??
I ignored it all because it seemed so *clichéd*! He said if I'd ever *asked*, he would have told me everything. But that's a lie. I *did* ask, and he lied every time.

RACHEL *cries again*.

He says he's a terrible liar. That's a lie. He does it for a living. I wish I had a *transcript*.
He's not *sorry*.

EDWARD. I'm sure he is.

RACHEL. He's sorry for *himself*. Not sorry for what he's done.

She drinks.

KITTY. Jake… You must be able to imagine how she feels? Put yourself in her shoes. You'd be feeling… I mean, how would *you* feel?

Beat.

JAKE. I wouldn't mind.

KITTY. Believe me, you would.

JAKE. No. She's right, when she says I'm not sorry. Because I'm not. I'm not sorry. I'm sorry she found *out* about it.

KITTY. You don't *regret* it?

JAKE. No. It was *good* for our marriage. It kept it alive. *She* says it's like I've brought a stranger into the house, it's a violation. But that's *retrospective*! Do you see what I mean? She didn't feel violated while I was actually *doing* it. It's only *now*.

KITTY. Jake – this is all – a bit – *legalistic*, isn't it?

EDWARD. Were you in *love*? With these women?

JAKE. No. Yes.

EDWARD. Well, yes or no?

JAKE. The answer isn't yes or no! The more you… make love with someone, the more you *make* love.

KITTY shifts on her feet, irritably.

KITTY. '*You*'?

JAKE. I mean me.

RACHEL. He's locked in *himself*. He's incapable of feeling guilt. He genuinely doesn't seem to see the difference between right and wrong…

She cries a little.

…he's so *fucking*…

KITTY. What do you want to happen?

RACHEL (*simply*). I want to hurt him.

EDWARD *turns back to* JAKE.

JAKE. I'm scared of her. I'm scared of what she might do.

EDWARD. But you *love* Rachel.

JAKE. Look at the way we got married.

RACHEL. He married me because I got pregnant.

JAKE. I'm very prone to feeling guilt. That was a major
motivating factor.
But when Jimmy was born...
It's like this. I've never liked Rachel's ears. She's got these
ears, they've got no lobes to them.
Jimmy was born and you know what – he's got those same
fucking ears! And I looked at them and I *loved* them.

He made me love *her* more...
...He made me love her more...

He weeps. EDWARD *embraces him.* KITTY *watches.*

Scene Six

TIM, EDWARD *and* ZARA *in a café.*

EDWARD. Basically, it's a fight. Between two opposing
narratives.

TIM. These are people in extreme situations.

EDWARD. There are a lot of chaotic facts and you want to pick
your way through and convince the jury of *one* simple line.

TIM. It's all about suggestion.

EDWARD. Make them see it from *your* client's point of view.

ZARA. Like *I* see things from my character's point of view.

TIM. Exactly.

EDWARD. So *what's* it called?

ZARA. *Wigging Out.* It'll be nine o'clock, BBC1. I'm up for a criminal barrister with no home life, speaks Mandarin and rollerblades –

EDWARD. Oh I know *loads* of them –

ZARA. – but I want to get the tone right.

TIM. Okay. So, say I'm prosecution, and he's – (EDWARD.) defence – I usually prosecute –

EDWARD. And lose.

TIM. Oh fuck you. I was *winning*, until I wasn't. I *knew* I'd lost the jury when I saw four of them had their arms folded. And actually, Ed, I think she *was* raped.

EDWARD. She was a complete pisshead who kept changing her story.

TIM. You fucking excluded the fact she *knew* he had previous for assault.

EDWARD. It was prejudicial! She should have said it in her statement, not five minutes before! Plus, she liked a bit of rough, if you looked at her previous boyfriends. *Anyway.* As the prosecution, Tim opens the case.

TIM. 'In this case you're going to hear from Zara…'

He indicates ZARA.

ZARA.…White.

TIM. 'Zara *White*, who alleges her genitals were grabbed by *this* man.' (*Pointing at* EDWARD.)

ZARA. Lovely.

TIM. Then I ask nice, open questions of you. Who, where, what why when. And you tell things from your point of view.

EDWARD. And then *I* fuck up that narrative.

TIM. You certainly do.

EDWARD. I cross-examine with closed questions.

ZARA. Closed questions?

EDWARD. Nasty questions where the choice is not genuine.
I pose a *different* point of view. (*He turns on* ZARA.)
'You *wanted* him to have sex with you, didn't you. Yes or
no? You asked him to fuck you blue, *didn't* you. Yes or no?'

He breaks off dreamily.

Do people say that? 'Fuck me blue'? It's been a long time…

ZARA. You do it *all* through questions?

TIM. Well, a question isn't always a question. A bald statement
can be *camouflaged* as a question. 'You're an arsehole,
really, aren't you, Ed.'

EDWARD. Look, what can I say! My rapist just performed a lot
better than your victim.

TIM. Probably because he'd had a lot of practice! She'd only
been raped the once –

EDWARD (*to* ZARA). The fact is we'd *both* cheat a five-year-
old at Tiddlywinks.

ZARA (*to* EDWARD). Kitty said you were doing lots of rapes
at the moment, which would be wonderful for me. Are there
any I could watch?

TIM. You don't want to watch him, you want to watch me! He's
human rights, what do you want to watch *him* for? Rape's
beneath him. *I'm* the one who does all the raping.

EDWARD. I'm not 'human rights', I'm just moving *in to*
human rights.

TIM. For the money –

EDWARD. What do you mean, 'the money', there is no money
in human rights –

TIM. There is when you're defending the human rights of
Google and BSkyB –

EDWARD. We need to look after their human rights too –

TIM. Despite the fact they're not human! (*To* ZARA.) He used to have ideals –

EDWARD. How else am I going to pay for our roof??

TIM. Do embarrassing regulatory work like the rest of us! License some minicabs and strip clubs!

EDWARD. Don't listen to him, he's actually in a very posh set where they cream off all the *fraud*, and that's why he lives in Camden and I live in Forest Hill.

ZARA. Try living in Enfield.

EDWARD (*obliviously*). Actually, as it happens, Tim, I *am* doing a couple more rapes. I've got to do a marital rape in Plymouth.

TIM. *Plymouth?*

EDWARD. Long story. I'm only doing it as a favour to Jake. Basically pro bono. Which if you know your Latin, means, paid fuck-all. (*To* ZARA.) Is all this any *use* to you?

TIM. We should be telling her how to stand, speak – and spectacles. Pick 'em up, put 'em down, they engage the listener when you're about to speak… And they make you look cleverer…

EDWARD. What about a parrot on your shoulder while you're at it?

TIM (*meaningfully*). Hmm. 'What about a parrot on your shoulder. While you're at it.' That's another one – repeat their answer slowly, like they've fucked up, and let it hang in the air.

EDWARD. Strictly for when you don't know what the hell else to do.

ZARA*'s phone rings*. EDWARD *reflexively checks his own phone*.

ZARA. Oh shit. It's my agent. I'll have to take this.

She picks up the phone.

Sarah! How's the *baby*??

She goes out. TIM *waits a split second, then –*

TIM. Back off!!

EDWARD (*looking up from his phone*)....I beg your pardon?

TIM. You're happily married, I'm a sad single bastard! Back off!

EDWARD. *What?*

TIM. You're flirting with her. Mr *Human Rights.*

EDWARD. I am not flirting!

TIM. Yes you are. Getting the conversation on to grabbing her genitals.

EDWARD. Actually, that was *you*, who got it on to grabbing her genitals, you said –

TIM. Oh it's all *subliminal.* Implying that it's a long time since you've slept with Kitty, fucking till you're blue – you fancy her rotten. Admit it.

EDWARD. No.

TIM. Don't you?

EDWARD. No. Absolutely not.

TIM. *Is* it a long time since you've had sex with Kitty?

EDWARD. None of your business.

TIM. Okay, so if you *don't* fancy her, and I'm wrong, you won't be embarrassed if I bring it up in front of her, then?

EDWARD. Look, she's a lovely girl, she's one of Kitty's oldest friends, and to be honest, I've always found her a bit pretentious.

TIM. That's neither here nor there when it comes to a blowjob. Seriously, Ed. Why are you keeping me off the grass?

EDWARD. Look, she wasn't interested.

TIM. What?

EDWARD....She wasn't interested in you. We tried to set you up. She wasn't interested. I'm sorry.

ZARA comes back in to the awkward pause.

ZARA. Fucking *babies*. Fascinating. Not. Sorry, this has been *so* useful. (*To* EDWARD.) I'd love to talk to you about the human-rights stuff, some time.

TIM. Don't, he'll be insufferable.

EDWARD. With pleasure.

ZARA is packing up her stuff, preparing to go.

ZARA. Thank you so much...

EDWARD. It was a pleasure.

TIM. Hang on. We've only done examination-in-chief. What about cross-examination?

Beat. He speaks without looking at EDWARD, *or* ZARA.

Because when you cross-examine you're not asking open questions any more. You're asking questions to draw attention to your case. To bend perceptions, to put an idea into the jury's mind. You fancy Zara, don't you, Ed?

Beat.

You give the answer in your question and that way you control the answer. You fancy Zara, don't you, Ed?

Beat.

Don't be afraid of silence. Use it to create tension.

Beat.

Or you can do it a different way. I suggest you fancy Zara, but you would disagree with me, wouldn't you?

Beat.

See, what I'm doing is, I'm putting my case. And by telling him he disagrees with it, I've closed him down to a yes or no answer. I've boxed him in.

Pause.

You fancy Zara.

EDWARD. No.

TIM. You engineered this session of research in order to have an excuse to flirt with her.

EDWARD. No.

TIM. Under the guise of advising Zara about a part in my presence you earned her confidence and ultimately your motive for doing so was to seduce her for yourself.

Beat.

This is bounce. I'm bouncing for confrontations. You get a rhythm going, you play dirty, you don't look at the witness but straight ahead, and you bounce your case off them. You're trying to get them to go 'It's a fair cop, guv.'

EDWARD. Which I'm not going to do.

TIM. The great thing is it doesn't matter if you do or you don't, Ed, because the *impression* is that it is a fair cop – you just can't admit it.

EDWARD. The other way is to create an embarrassment. We call this looking for the lever. Do you find my wife attractive, Tim?

Pause.

Do you find my wife attractive, Tim?

TIM. No.

EDWARD. You're saying my wife is not attractive, am I right?

TIM. No.

EDWARD. So she *is* an attractive woman, my wife, you would say, Tim?

TIM. Yes.

EDWARD. And yet *you* don't find her attractive, is that right?

Pause.

You said earlier my wife *is* an attractive woman. Then you say you don't find her attractive. Which is the lie?

See? It's a sort of trapdoor. You ring-fence around, locking off escape routes. And then you pull the lever. You drive an unanswerable rhetorical wedge between the answers.

TIM *looks at* EDWARD.

TIM. Fuck you.

He exits.

ZARA. Bloody hell!

EDWARD. Oh, he's just cross because he lost the case.
It was *tennis*.

ZARA. It was *boxing*!

Beat. They look at one another.

EDWARD. I'd be very happy to talk to you about the human-rights stuff. Another time.

ZARA. I'd love that.

EDWARD. And good luck with the audition.

ZARA. Oh someone else got it.

EDWARD. What?

ZARA. That's why my agent rang.

EDWARD. Oh no!

ZARA. Story of my life. But I'd still love to hear about the human rights.

They smile at each other.

Scene Seven

TIM *and* KITTY *stand in* TIM*'s house. The furniture is covered with dust sheets. The space feels bigger than* KITTY *and* EDWARD*'s house.* TIM *looks at* KITTY *questioningly.*

TIM. …Can you feel it?

KITTY *stands, as if listening. She looks up, takes in the space.*

KITTY. Um…

She moves around a little. Stops.

Can I *feel* anything… I don't *think*…

I don't *think* I can… I don't think I can feel anything… no…

Pause. TIM *continues to look at* KITTY *questioningly. They stand looking at each other, a little way apart.*

I mean, what exactly am I meant to be feeling?

TIM. I don't know.

Beat.

Stupid really: I just thought…

No, but…?

…I just get this *feeling.*

KITTY. Like… there's *someone else*?

TIM. Yes.

Pause.

Do you know what I mean?… The upstairs landing, I was looking around it, and I found these… marks low down on the wall.

KITTY. What kind of marks?

TIM. Little… it looked like little finger marks.

KITTY. Hand marks?

TIM. Like someone with very small hands.

KITTY.... Well, maybe...

TIM. Low down on the wall.

KITTY. Maybe it was some child who lived here before.

TIM. But I'd just had it painted.

Beat.

KITTY. Hmmm. I'm sorry, I'm not being very helpful, am I?

TIM. No, no... I don't know why I'm getting so – it's ridiculous, I just wanted a second opinion. Or something. I don't know why I texted.

KITTY. No, it's fine, it's fine.

TIM. Yeah well I just thought... Do you want some tea?

He busies himself. KITTY *looks at her phone.*

What are they meant to *be*, anyway? Poltergeists?

KITTY. I don't know. A destructive force, I suppose.

TIM. I'd offer you a biscuit but all my food tastes vaguely of *cupboard*... don't know why.

KITTY *looks around.*

KITTY. God, you've got so much *space* here!... Ed's 'study' is like flying Ryanair, I worry about him getting deep vein thrombosis.

TIM. My architect keeps asking where I want to put the nursery. For my phantom children.

KITTY *inspects the sofa, which is covered in a sheet.*

KITTY. Tim. You should move this *here*. So it's facing the window.

TIM *looks at it, as if for the first time.*

TIM. You think?

KITTY. Yes.

They take hold of the sofa and swivel it to a different position. As they do so:

You know our sofas have been sitting there for months. Ed and I just can't agree on where to put them.

TIM. But you guys are great at communicating.

KITTY. We're not great at communicating. We just always agree. When we don't agree, we're fucked…

TIM. To the left a bit?

KITTY. Sure… And Ed's infuriatingly *logical*, which just winds me up… 'Well how come you "just don't like" the sofa there, Kitty? You're an intelligent person, aren't you?…'

TIM. Unfortunately cross-examination is a very damaging form of communication…

KITTY. He's so good at dressing his opinion up as comment.

TIM. 'You may think, members of the jury, this is a sofa you cannot trust. That is a matter for *you*.'

They exert themselves with the sofa.

…Where is he now?

KITTY (*breathlessly*). With Jake.

TIM. Oh God, Jake.

KITTY. Yes, Jake. It's reached crisis point. Ed's on Jake's side. I'm on Rachel's.

TIM. I thought you were on Jake's side.

KITTY. That was before I *heard* Jake's side.

TIM.… What *I* keep wondering is – why do people *do* it?

KITTY. I *couldn't*. Never. I like the moral high-ground too much, for a start.

TIM. I suppose I just find it very hard to imagine.

KITTY. Well so do I! Why would you *behave* like that?

TIM. No, what I meant was, you know, what *is* being unfaithful? When does it start?

Beat. They look at the sofa.

Is meeting an ex and not telling being unfaithful?
Is *thinking* about it being unfaithful?
…Is *dreaming* about someone being unfaithful?

When does it start?

KITTY. You know what I think? When people talk about it. The more people *talk* about it, the more they end up actually doing it.

TIM. That is true.

KITTY *is looking at the sofa.*

KITTY. I'm astounded by the lack of insight, the way people don't seem to *see* what they're doing even as they're doing it.

TIM. People are amazingly suggestible.

KITTY. The level of denial. (*The sofa.*) – That's much better.

TIM *gives her a cup of tea.*

TIM. How was the holiday?

KITTY. Exhausting… Do you know, I never thought I'd say this, but I actually miss work.

TIM. Even the crazy fucking authors?

KITTY. Even the crazy fucking authors, *even* the fucking blurbs! God, I spent *hours* on them, mini-masterpieces. Changing 'a' for 'the' and back again. Those were the days.

They laugh.

…I'm so glad we've only got one.

TIM. You don't want more?

KITTY. No. Ed does. But it would be the end of our relationship.

TIM *laughs.*

Luckily, he can't impregnate me by force.
He tries, sweetly.
Anyway, how's *your* love-life?

TIM. Oh... Jesus... it's exhausting... *Dates*... having to take my patter out for the night... So draining. Afterwards I have to lie down in a darkened room. Alone.

KITTY fans herself.

KITTY. So bloody hot, isn't it? Our bedroom is about thirty degrees at the moment.

She looks around the room again.

Why the hell we put it in the attic...

TIM. Because the view is fantastic.

KITTY. The heat gives me nightmares.

TIM. Me too! What about?

KITTY....I dream... the dream is very very ordinary... but I just dream...

Pause.

I dream... that I'm unhappily married...

And then I wake up and I remember that I'm married to Ed, and it's all okay.

There is silence. They look at each other.

What?

TIM (*intently*). There. Do you feel it now?

Pause.

Do you feel something?

They look at each other, intently.

Kitty...?

KITTY. Yes...

I feel something, yes...

They stare at each other. Scared.

Scene Eight

KITTY *is sitting at the kitchen table. She is fiddling with her phone. A door slams from off.* EDWARD *enters, in his coat, opening a box of French Fancies. He walks straight through and out, comes back on no longer wearing his coat, eating a French Fancy, goes straight off again, shouts from off.*

EDWARD (*off*). Is he asleep?

KITTY. Well, she's dropping proceedings.

EDWARD (*off*). What?

KITTY. Yep. I just saw her.

EDWARD (*off*). She's dropping proceedings?

KITTY. Yep. And Jake's moving back in.

EDWARD *comes back in, chewing.*

Can you believe it?

EDWARD. I know.

KITTY. You know?

EDWARD. Well, I practically brokered the deal. Not wanting to boast or anything.

Fantastic! Why don't we have a vodka to celebrate?

KITTY. We don't have anything to drink it with.

He goes out of the room to get a bottle of vodka. Shouts from off. Meanwhile KITTY *looks at her phone.*

EDWARD. Is there *anything* that isn't improved by mixing it with vodka? – Actually, no, let me answer that. Sugar Puffs. And I should know. You are looking at one brilliant negotiator here. Talk about the art of persuasion!

KITTY (*flatly*). I don't want one.

EDWARD *comes back in with the vodka bottle.*

EDWARD. What?

KITTY. I don't want one.
  She's making a huge mistake.

EDWARD. Who?

KITTY. Rachel. Is making a huge mistake. Taking him back.

  Beat.

EDWARD. I hope you didn't *say* that to her.

KITTY. Of course not. I said I understood. I don't.

EDWARD. What do *you* think she should do?

KITTY. Leave him.

  Beat.

EDWARD (*taken aback*). Kit, she was going to run *conduct*.
  It was insane. As a barrister, she should know better.

KITTY. She wasn't *thinking* as a barrister, she was hurting and
  wanted her side of the story to be heard!

EDWARD. That's what dinner parties are for! If it isn't about
  him spending their *cash*, which he wasn't, they don't care!

KITTY. Why did you persuade her to stay? Do you actually
  think they're *better* together?

EDWARD. Taking him to court wouldn't have got her
  anywhere.

KITTY. Will you stop being so fucking *detached* for once??

EDWARD. Saying 'You don't have to put up with this' is
  actually pretty bad advice!

KITTY. Jake has done something wrong and I think he should
  be punished and he should say sorry!

EDWARD. He *has* said sorry!

KITTY. But he doesn't *mean* it!

EDWARD. It's very difficult to *mean* an apology if it's
  demanded from you.

KITTY. Do you know what? You have *never* said sorry to me in your life.

Beat.

EDWARD. That is not true.

KITTY. It *is*. It took you a long time to say I love you. A long time to say will you marry me. But you've *never* said I'm sorry. Because saying sorry is an admission of guilt. You told me, Ed, when you were a kid you would only ever say 'I apologise' – and *that's* why you became a barrister.

Beat.

EDWARD. Sorry, I'm *completely* lost. Should *I* be the one saying sorry? For Jake cheating on Rachel? She was being *mad*!

KITTY. What if *I* cheated on *you*? How do you think *you* would feel?

EDWARD....I wouldn't go mad.

KITTY. How do you *know*?

EDWARD. Because it wouldn't *get* me anywhere!

KITTY. It's not about *getting* somewhere! That's not *why* people go mad!! It's not a *tactical* move, Ed! Even a *child* could see what Jake has done is wrong –

EDWARD. Bullshit, children see things from *one* point of view, their own, just introduce a box of Smarties –

KITTY. If Jake had an ounce of *empathy*, if he could see how he was making Rachel feel –

During the following, KITTY *tries and fails to interject – until* EDWARD *reaches his full stop.*

EDWARD. Not empathy, not that old fucking chestnut, please –

KITTY. Ed –

EDWARD. – I'm so sick of hearing that word invoked! I'm tired, I've been listening to bollocks all day long in court, victim's *impact* statements –

KITTY. Wait –

EDWARD. – people going on about what they think is fair after two Chardonnays and now *I* want a drink –

KITTY. Ed!!

EDWARD. – and you know what, the last thing I feel is empathy.

Finally –

KITTY. Okay. No, go on, Ed. I want to know. What's the *argument* against empathy? You've really stumped me.

EDWARD. All right! It's completely *innumerate*, for a start.

KITTY. *Innumerate?*

EDWARD. Yes. A genocide doesn't get as much airtime as one little boy killed and hidden in someone's attic.

KITTY. I see.

EDWARD. And empathy's not actually *fair*. You're only feeling for Rachel. Not Jake.

KITTY. We saw her, crying, in this kitchen –

EDWARD. We saw him crying in this kitchen. He wasn't faking it –

KITTY. No, no he wasn't faking it. He was *genuinely* self-pitying!

EDWARD. You don't want people with their heart in the right place, you want people with their *brain* in the right place –

KITTY. Ed, if you have no empathy, then we are fucked!

EDWARD. I don't need to have experienced something to have an opinion on it!

KITTY (*shouting*). You do! You do, you do, you do!

As she shouts, she picks up the kettle and hurls it at him.

EDWARD (*shocked*). Jesus Christ, Kitty!

In the stunned silence.

KITTY. *You've never had it done to you*.
You've *cheated*.
You've never been cheated on.
You'll never know what it's like until it happens to you.
That's the only way you'll ever understand.

She walks out.

Scene Nine

EDWARD *and* KITTY's *kitchen. Much laughter. A drunken atmosphere, fast and loud.* ZARA, TIM, JAKE, RACHEL, EDWARD *and* KITTY *are all there.* KITTY *and* EDWARD *stay physically apart from one another.* ZARA *and* TIM *are tactile with one another.* RACHEL *and* JAKE *are also tactile with one another.* EDWARD *is pouring wine.* ZARA *is trying to complete a statement. Many conversations happening at once.* JAKE *has opened a box of crackers.*

ZARA. Look –

EDWARD (*generally*). Who wants more?

KITTY (*to* EDWARD). How many have you *had*?

JAKE. *Please* can we pull the crackers?

EDWARD (*to* KITTY). I haven't been *counting*.

KITTY (*to* JAKE). Do we *have* to? Can't we leave it till later?

EDWARD. I don't pull crackers! For religious reasons!

   JAKE *starts handing out crackers.*

JAKE. Crackers! Ecologically sound crackers!

   ZARA *readies herself to pull her cracker with* EDWARD.
   Around her, others do the same. KITTY *holding her cracker on her own.*

KITTY. Wait, who's going to pull with me?

JAKE. I will. (*Takes hold of one end of the cracker and braces himself.*)
Come on, everybody. Enforced fun, coming up.
One – two – *three*!

They all pull. The crackers refuse to come apart. They strain.

EDWARD. Jesus!

JAKE. …Fucking *hell*.

RACHEL. What are these *made* of? *Lino?*

They strain. Slowly, some of them come apart – without bangs.

JAKE. Ecologically sound. One-hundred-per-cent recycled.

EDWARD. Short on the bangs, aren't they.

After more straining, the rest come apart.

RACHEL. Bloody *hell*. (*Inspects inside the cracker.*) What have we got here?

She holds it up.

A pencil. That's very…

ZARA (*holds up another pencil*). I was hoping for jewellery.

JAKE unfolds a joke.

JAKE. Ooh, look – !

He reads aloud, puzzled.

'Is your water too hot? Your thermostat shouldn't need to be set higher than sixty degrees celsius.'

RACHEL. It's the way you tell them.

KITTY. There are hats.

They put on the hats.

JAKE. A festive toast! To me! To Rachel!
To *marriage*!

EDWARD (*raising glass*). To Love!

The others echo the toast absent-mindedly.

Actually… (*Stands up*.) I'd like to make a little speech…

RACHEL. Oh God…

EDWARD.…I'd just like to say, Rachel, Jake –

RACHEL. No…

EDWARD.…How happy I am, that you are both here… tonight… my oldest, crappiest friend and his dear wife…

KITTY. Stop it, you'll make them self-conscious…

EDWARD. I can't believe that, many many years ago, I wore this same waistcoat to your *wedding*… And here you are today…

JAKE. Still married…

RACHEL. Only just…

JAKE. Well, you never know who's going to last the course…

EDWARD. So I would like to toast you, in *this*, my wedding waistcoat…

ZARA. Yes, it's a bit shiny, isn't it…

EDWARD. What are you talking about… this is my *wedding* waistcoat…

JAKE. Let *me* put on the wedding waistcoat… and I'll renew my vows…

EDWARD. Stop hijacking my bloody toast!! To Rachel and Jake.

Everyone echoes the toast.

JAKE. Seriously. Let me put the wedding waistcoat on and *I'll* make a toast.

EDWARD *starts to take the waistcoat off,* JAKE *to put it on.*

RACHEL. Oh my God, this is going to be like the worst Chippendales *ever*…

JAKE. To my wife. To forgiveness! To marriage! It's like the law! It's flawed, but it's all we've got!

RACHEL. All right, all right.

JAKE. To Kitty and Edward, solid as a rock! And to new love! To Zara, to Tim!

ZARA. Thank you!

They all drink again.

RACHEL.…Can we just *talk* now?

EDWARD (*grandly*). You may speak.

KITTY. How was your romantic weekend?

TIM/ZARA. Fantastic.

ZARA. We decided against skiing.

TIM. The last time I took a girlfriend skiing… quite early on in the relationship, I might add…

JAKE. Bold.

TIM.…I fell all the way down a difficult run, bruised my chest very badly… and the bruises, the bruised *blood* gradually made its way *down* my chest until it collected… in my penis. Which turned black.

EDWARD. Finally you had a big black cock.

TIM (*modestly*). Well I would never confidently say *big*.

ZARA (*to* EDWARD). So what *is* your case?

EDWARD. Oh God, I really don't want to talk about it.

KITTY. Makes a change.

EDWARD. It's a historic rape. Fills me with weariness just to say it.

EDWARD *is busying himself with a joint.*

JAKE. Oh, I have a bit of a problem with them.

EDWARD. Me too.

KITTY. Why?

EDWARD. Well, if someone steals a *watch* off me ten years ago, I have to have some evidence, but with rape, it seems like *anyone* can have a go, bringing it up *now* as an alibi for their failed life.

JAKE. I'd love to have an alibi for *my* failed life.

RACHEL. You do. Your penis.

TIM. Do we *have* to talk about rape? It's not very Christmassy.

EDWARD (*to* ZARA). Rachel is a very brilliant prosecutor of sex crimes. Rape, incest, child sex abuse – you name it.

ZARA. Wow.

RACHEL. The *best* fun I've ever had outside the bedroom is cross-examining defendants. You can tie them in a gentle and lovely knot if you take the time to craft it.

JAKE. I thought that's what you did *inside* the bedroom.

RACHEL. Ha ha.

EDWARD (*with finality*). Oh God, in my experience, the *victims* are never completely innocent either. I'm fed up with them. They're all mad. No smoke without fire. They're like the weird bullied people at school.

A general outcry headed by RACHEL.

RACHEL. Ed, that's outrageous!!

EDWARD. No, I'm honestly losing faith in the whole system. I don't believe in argument any more, I don't think people listen to argument, rationality, logic – they just *decide*, and that's that.

ZARA. Oh *Ed*.

KITTY. Take no notice. He's always like this when he's just lost a case. Or three.

JAKE. Ed!

RACHEL. The last *three*?

TIM. What happened to the old Midas Touch?

ZARA (*to* EDWARD). What were the cases?

EDWARD. One about a Tamil stabbing his wife...
He ran off to the Bahamas and came back with a tattoo on his arm that said 'Forgive and forget' –

He picks up a knife, gestures vaguely.

It all hinged on which hand the alleged –

TIM. I think you mean convicted –

EDWARD. All right, all right – on which hand the bloody *convicted* used for stabbing and the angle... difficult to describe without showing you...

ZARA. Stab me, stab me!

EDWARD. It's all right, Zara... and he had a fucking long name which I kept forgetting –

RACHEL. Why didn't you use the Tamil's street name?

EDWARD. Because it was Psycho, bit prejudicial – it always comes down to phone records with these crims you know, they *never* turn their phone off, you'd think they'd learn... haven't they watched *The Wire*... these people with their chaotic fucking *lives*...

KITTY. Says God.

EDWARD. I don't think I'm God.

TIM. Right, so you *often* think, 'That could be me.'

EDWARD. I do. With the careless drivers, absolutely. Less with the rapists and the gang-related stabbings.

KITTY. You say 'I' and 'we' when you're defending them but it's not, it's *them*, isn't it?

EDWARD. Yes, it's them, and so what? We're *not* them! That's why we're paid to *argue* for them – because they can't string two fucking words together!

ZARA. You don't feel for them?

EDWARD. Why should I?

KITTY. Because you bloody pretend to!

EDWARD. Because it helps my case!

KITTY. And you wonder why you keep losing!!

Someone lets out an 'Oooh!'

EDWARD. All right, tell me. Why do I keep losing? And why do you keep *needling* me?

Beat.

KITTY. Okay, do you want to hear what I think, Ed? Being married to you for ten years?

EDWARD (*picking up a knife*). Yes, go ahead. I'll just point out I am holding a knife.

KITTY *pauses, picks up a knife too, the others laugh.*

KITTY. I think you've been doing this job for too long. Dealing with dishonest, violent, sexually odd people day after day.

RACHEL. And that's just Jake.

KITTY. Standing up and lying in front of people. It corrupts you. And like all people who know that they're clever, you're actually slightly stupid.

JAKE. She's got a point.

KITTY. You're so used to being adversarial, you can't hear anything without immediately taking the opposite point of view. You've developed a skill for closing off your mind.

EDWARD. Or shall we just get divorced?

KITTY. You know that pedantic logic that barristers use? 'Why did you carry on living with your stepfather if he raped you, it doesn't make sense?' The only time anyone uses that pedantic logic in *life*, is when they're denying having an affair.

A sudden pause.

'What do you mean, I'm shagging my clerk. It wouldn't make sense. I'd be risking everything.'

No one knows what to say.

Yes, you have skills. You have a hugely overdeveloped short-term memory – you can become an expert on *tyre* mechanics in a very short space of time – but then you shed it like a skin –

JAKE. Interesting you use a reptilian image –

KITTY. And consequently you have no long-term memory at all.

EDWARD. So?

KITTY. You conveniently forget anything you've ever done wrong.

RACHEL. Hear, hear.

EDWARD *pointedly puts his knife down. They laugh.*

EDWARD. Having no long-term memory is great, Kitty, it means I don't hold on to grudges.

EDWARD *gets up on a chair.*

KITTY. What are you doing?

EDWARD. I'm taking the moral high-ground. First off. What you call 'picky points'. You're looking for the ring of truth in a witness's account. So you've *got* to test it. And consistency is a hallmark of truth.

KITTY. Crap! That logic *only* works in court. You test people with logic, but in life we act illogically all the time.

ZARA (*eagerly*). It's the mark of being a human –

KITTY (*ignoring her*). Inconsistency could be a mark of *truth*, consistency could be a hallmark of *lying*. 'You've got your story and you're sticking to it.'

RACHEL. It's true, if two witnesses give exactly the same account, they're probably lying.

EDWARD. If a witness gives a very detailed, consistent account they're probably telling the truth.

KITTY. Okay, why don't we play truth or dare?

Beat.

RACHEL. Oh, I *love* truth or dare.

ZARA. No, the hat game, the hat game.

KITTY. No, truth or dare.

JAKE. Oh God, I *hate* truth or dare.

KITTY. Let's start with Ed. Truth or dare?

Beat. EDWARD *gets down from the chair.*

EDWARD. All right. Truth.

KITTY. Where were you yesterday at 3.15 in the afternoon?

Beat.

EDWARD. I was at Chambers. Then I went for a drink with Alex.

KITTY. Why didn't you answer your mobile when I called?

JAKE. You're only allowed one question, right?

EDWARD (*ignoring him*). Because it was on silent.

KITTY. When did you see that I had called?

Beat.

EDWARD. About two hours later.

KITTY. So you didn't look at your mobile phone for two whole hours?

EDWARD. Yes.

Pause.

KITTY. Tell the truth.

EDWARD. I have.

KITTY. I dare you to tell the truth.

EDWARD. I have.

Pause.

ZARA. Well, *that* was weird.

EDWARD. No no no. Don't we all get to ask questions?

RACHEL. That's right, you do.

EDWARD. Kitty. Truth or dare.

KITTY. Truth.

Beat.

EDWARD. All right, Kitty. You say I've never said sorry to you.

KITTY. You never have.

EDWARD. Have you ever *really* forgiven me?

Beat.

KITTY. No.

Pause.

EDWARD. Well. Now I know.

Pause.

JAKE. *I've* got a question. Can we not play truth or dare?

RACHEL. No, *I've* got a question. What happens if you don't tell the truth in truth and dare?

KITTY. Nothing.

Beat. JAKE stands on a chair.

JAKE. Your honour, I have tried to stay off my feet. But now *I'm* going to take the moral high-ground. Please don't let's play any more truth or dare, it's ghastly.

RACHEL. No, I want a go, actually.

JAKE. (Why do I bother?)

RACHEL. Kitty, truth or dare?

KITTY. Truth.

TIM. Isn't *anyone* going to choose dare?

RACHEL. What have you never forgiven Edward for?

Beat.

KITTY. For having an affair.

Pause.

ZARA. Guys, guys, guys, stop it.

EDWARD. It doesn't mean I'm having one now.

KITTY. No. It means I haven't forgiven you.

Pause.

EDWARD. What do I have to do?

KITTY. All you have to do is say, unconditionally –
Sorry, I was wrong.

Beat.

But you can't resist arguing back. Can you?

EDWARD. What do you want to do about it?

KITTY. Make you feel what it's like.

Pause. The doorbell rings.

JAKE. Christ.

RACHEL. I'll get it.

*RACHEL gets up and goes out to the front door. The rest are
still, looking and not looking at one another. There are some
murmured voices from off.*

RACHEL comes back in.

Ed. There's a woman. She says she's here to see you?

EDWARD. Who is it?

RACHEL. She –

*But GAYLE has already come into the room. She stands
there. GAYLE looks at EDWARD. Long pause. She looks
at TIM.*

GAYLE. You're *both* here?

Beat.

So you're *mates*?

EDWARD *stands up*.

EDWARD. Sorry, can I help you?

GAYLE *looks around*.

GAYLE. Been drinking, have you?

Beat.

EDWARD. Do you want to go into the next room?

GAYLE. No, I dinnae want to go 'into the next room'.

Beat.

EDWARD. Why are you here?

GAYLE. Why d'you think?

Beat.

You fucked me up, pal.

EDWARD. Wait a second –

GAYLE. No no no, you dinnae get to tell me to 'pause' now.

(*To* TIM.) And *you* – *you* were fucking useless.

TIM. I'm sorry –

GAYLE. Yeah, you're right there, I'm sorry an' all.

Beat.

EDWARD. I think we should go next door –

But simultaneously ZARA *gets up in an attempt to offer* GAYLE *her seat*.

ZARA. Can I – ?

But GAYLE *overrides her*.

GAYLE. Why wasn't I allowed to say that he beat up my friend when she dumped him? That he stamped on her thigh and broke it, that he was already on bail for that?

TIM. Yes –

GAYLE. I'm speaking! That's why I *answered* his fucking text. I didne want him to come *back* and do *me* in. But they told me I cannae say anything about his 'past'. I didn't get to say any of that. I wasne *allowed*. You *promised* me I'd get to say all that in court. All I did was waste my time telling that stupid woman with her stupid notebook.

Beat.

EDWARD. Yes… that's because he's, that was correct, an application was made to the judge but it was decided he would be tried on the facts of the case alone.

GAYLE. What about me? What about bringin' up my mental health? So you bring my past in to it but not his? How is that fair?

Beat.

I didne even *want* to go to court.

For a moment she is suddenly near tears, then angry again.

Who was defending *me*?

TIM. Well, unfortunately having therapy –

He looks at EDWARD. EDWARD *takes over.*

EDWARD. Unfortunately having therapy can… undermine your case.

GAYLE. You have *got* to be joking me, you're talking *mince* here! Having therapy undermines my case?? And he – (EDWARD.) can make a prick out of me for it?

EDWARD. I'm sorry –

GAYLE. Yeah, and then yer erse fell off. Oh dry yer eyes, you're no '*sorry*', don't give me that shite. I saw yer face, didn't I? You were right *chuffed*. You *won*.

Beat.

EDWARD. Look –

GAYLE. Don't tell me it wasne personal. It was personal for *me*, pal.

She looks around the room. Addresses the others.

This interesting to ye?

This lot, they your mates?

ZARA *takes a step towards* GAYLE.

ZARA. Would you like a drink?
Can we at least get you a drink?

But GAYLE *is looking at* KITTY.

GAYLE. She your wife?

No one says anything.

(*To* KITTY.) How long you been with him then?

Beat.

Yeah, so I know where you live. (*To* EDWARD.) It was easy, following you. You *never* stop looking at your phone, do you. I know where you live and you dinnae like that, do you.

Well you know what, *Patrick Taylor* knows where *I* live. So now you know what it feels like, eh?

Beat.

EDWARD. Look. Unfortunately, Gayle, unfortunately for you, we presume innocence, because better a guilty man goes free than an innocent go to jail.

GAYLE. Why? Who says that's better?

JAKE. The law, for Christ's sake.

RACHEL. Do you feel you –

GAYLE. You don't look so happy either, babes, I'll tell you that for free.

TIM. Look. An injustice took place –

But GAYLE *is sniffing the air, suddenly interrupts him.*

GAYLE. You been smoking?

No one answers.

Yeah, you've been smoking *weed*. Christ, I cannae believe that it was in your hands. He – (TIM.) met me for the first time five minutes before and then I had to watch you fight it out, what a fucking *mess*.

EDWARD. It might have helped if you hadn't turned up drunk on the second day.

TIM. Ed, Ed, Ed. Shush. (*To* GAYLE.) I understand you must feel –

EDWARD. No, let me finish, the law's not going to work according to your emotions, Gayle, because it's got to be dispassionate, it's got to be impersonal –

GAYLE. But it *wasn't*.

EDWARD. – it's *not* about satisfying your personal sense of outrage, because if it *was*, it wouldn't be *fair* and that is the whole fucking point. I'm not going to apologise for the fact that I'm friends with him and I'm not going to apologise for cross-examining you.

GAYLE *looks at him coolly.*

GAYLE. What you did to me was criminal.

Pause. She turns to go. She turns back.

You know what. You don't even know *why* I was having therapy.

EDWARD. No, I don't.

GAYLE. 'Cause I was *raped*, that's why. Years ago. Before Patrick Taylor. Ten years ago. Me and my sister hitchhiking, two blokes, picked us up and took us to the woods. They did us side by side.
That's why I was *having* therapy. Ten years later. *Because* I was raped.

She goes to the door. Stops.

I held her hand while it was going on.

Suddenly, she starts to cry. KITTY *goes to her. Tries to hold her.*

KITTY. I'm sorry.

GAYLE. Don't *touch* me.

GAYLE *cries.*

Interval.

ACT TWO

Scene One

EDWARD *sits in the kitchen at his laptop. There is a pile of legal papers beside him, with the pink ribbons around them, and his phone nearby.* KITTY *comes in from outside.*

KITTY. God, it's hot out there.

They look at each other.

EDWARD. Listen to this windbag.

He opens a paper, reads brightly as if it is a children's story.

'Phone records. Frequent calls between one number and another may tell you something of the relationship. If there is a pattern of calls and then it stops, it may suggest that the two are together. If there are calls that don't get through it might tell you that the person doesn't want to be located...' Jeez, he's thorough, I'll give him that. Even the accused looked bored in the dock.

EDWARD *gets up, goes out. She looks after him.*

KITTY. Is he asleep?

No answer. KITTY *goes to the laptop. Looks at it. Moves off, takes off her jacket.*

EDWARD *comes back in.*

EDWARD. Where were you?

KITTY. With Michelle.

EDWARD. I called you.

He sits back down at his laptop. KITTY *gets her phone out.*

KITTY. Oh, it was on silent.

Was it anything important?

Beat.

EDWARD. The bedroom smells funny.

KITTY. Does it?

Beat.

What of?

EDWARD. Football boots.

KITTY. I told you that. Months ago. You said I was imagining it.

EDWARD. There's a smudge on the wall.

By the headboard.

KITTY. Is there?

EDWARD. Or a stain.

KITTY. Maybe it's a poltergeist.

Beat.

EDWARD. Why have you been calling Tim?

Beat.

KITTY. I haven't been calling him.

EDWARD. Really?

KITTY. Yes.

EDWARD. I called Tim this afternoon. He didn't answer.

Beat.

Why don't we see if he answers your call?

Call him.

KITTY. What?

Pause.

EDWARD. Okay, I'll call him.

He takes out his mobile phone, selects a number.

Waits.

Terminates the call.

Now you call him.

KITTY. No.

EDWARD. Why not?

KITTY. Because he's going to think it's fucking weird. You're being fucking weird.

Pause.

KITTY *silently selects the number off her phone.*

Waits.

Someone picks up at the other end.

Hi, Tim. It's Kitty.

Beat. She laughs.

Yeah, I know, sorry to bother you.

I'm just ringing because Ed thinks I'm having an affair with you.

Pause. She laughs.

Well, sorry about that.

Enjoy the cricket.

Okay. Take care.

Bye.

She terminates the call.

EDWARD *and* KITTY *stare at each other.*

EDWARD. It's him, isn't it.

KITTY. What are you *talking* about? You're being a prat.

EDWARD. It's him.

Beat.

I looked at your phone. It's empty. No texts, no call records.

KITTY. I decluttered it.

Beat.

There's a lot of wine left open from the other night. We should throw it away.

EDWARD. I haven't cheated on you for five years.

KITTY. Congratulations. What anniversary is that? Ruby? Oh no, I forgot, it's *tin*.

EDWARD. I'm guilty or guilty. Either I've been cheating on you and I deserve punishment or I cheated on you five years ago and deserve punishment.

Beat.

KITTY. Can we just run this by ourselves? I've known Tim for *nearly* ten years. I've never fancied him. He's been single all this time. Why would I start having an affair with him *now*, when he's with Zara –

EDWARD. 'Why would I do it, I'd be risking everything, it doesn't make sense.' Because he saw his chance and he fucking took it.

KITTY. Fuck *you*, Ed. Stop being fucking poisonous.

EDWARD. Yeah. That's a really good one. The power of being *offended*. It's sort of unanswerable. Own up to your fucking feelings. You're bored. You don't want to have sex with me any more.

KITTY. I split myself in *two* for you and that fucking baby, don't *ever* try and guilt trip me –

EDWARD. Why won't you give me another child?

Pause.

When did you start sleeping with your back to me?
Why won't you ever face me, in bed?
If you're doing this to hurt me, I don't get why you're *lying*?

Silence.

I don't believe this. He's one of those boring men. I don't
know where they make them but there must be a factory
somewhere. Near fucking Norwich.

I mean, *why*??
When?

When I was in New York?

For fuck's sake, spit it out.

KITTY. When do you think I would have had time? Why would
I want to do it? Where would we have done it? – Or would
you rather *closed* questions? I wanted to do it to get my own
back, didn't I. I wanted to see if I could, isn't that right. I can
do it too, Ed.

EDWARD. Look at you. Finding all these arguments. You
wanted to do it so you did it.

KITTY. All right!!
How about *I wanted you to understand how it felt*.

Pause.

EDWARD. That *is* a miscarriage of justice.

KITTY. I *knew* you were going to say that.

Pause.

EDWARD. You're nuts.

KITTY. No, I'm not.

EDWARD. Are you serious? You did it to punish me? Five
years late?

KITTY (*quietly*). Yes.

Beat.

EDWARD. No. If you're *punishing* me, why didn't you *tell* me?

Pause.

I'm trying to understand, Kit, I'm really trying to understand, but if it was some kind of *victim's justice*, show the criminal how the crime made you feel, why bother hiding it?

KITTY. Because I felt *guilty*!

EDWARD. Why?

Beat.

You're not in *love* with him, are you?

Beat.

Well that's fucked things up, hasn't it. That's not *fair*, is it.

You know what. You haven't been *here*. For weeks.
You've already gone.
That's why the bedroom feels empty.
He's stolen you, the fucking *thief*.
Christ.
I want to be *sick*.

He bends over, breathes heavily.

He starts to cry.

KITTY. I'm sorry.

Beat.

Ed…

He straightens up. He takes her in his arms. She resists.

EDWARD. Please.

She lets him hold her.

Please.

He starts to take her clothes off. She resists.

He cries.

I put the thought in his head.

KITTY (*gently*). No. You put the thought in *my* head.

EDWARD. Please. Let me.

   I apologise. I apologise.

   KITTY *is crying too*.

KITTY. No. It's too late.

   Lights fade on them.

Scene Two

JAKE, RACHEL *and* EDWARD *sit together. Their
configuration should echo the scene in the first act when* JAKE
came to KITTY *and* EDWARD, *but now it is* EDWARD *who is
dishevelled and* JAKE *and* RACHEL *who listen
sympathetically.* EDWARD *is a wreck. Mid-flow.*

EDWARD. I told her, if you're feeling confused, spending time
   apart is *not* going to make you *less* confused. She said I've
   got no feelings, that I'm cold. That I see everything from an
   intellectual point of view, that I have no emotions.

   He weeps, buries his head in a hankie, blows his nose loudly.

   Christ. I haven't cried like this since prep school.

JAKE. And Tim?

EDWARD (*hoarsely*). *Cunt.* I want to kill him. With my bare
   hands. I have these dreams where I'm shouting at him and then
   I grab his hands and – (*Gesturing.*) I *tear* his fingers apart –

JAKE. Yes, yes yes but has he left Zara?

EDWARD. Of course he has!

RACHEL. Where's Kitty now?

EDWARD. They're at his place. (*His voice rises again.*) He'll
   steal my fucking *child*, the fucking… I'm not leaving! I told

her she'd have to divorce me first. I'm not leaving the
fucking house. She can fuck off. She can sleep in the fucking
shed if she wants to stay. She's left. If she's in love with him,
she can fucking fuck the fuck off, if she wants to fight me for
Leo, she can.

RACHEL. She won't fight you for Leo.

EDWARD. Christ. 'I'm in *love*.' People use the word love like
'Hitler'. Let's see how fucking great she feels about being in
love when I've got Leo –

RACHEL. Slow down, slow down,

JAKE. Tell us what actually *happened*.

EDWARD. It... I... she... can fuck off...
    ...I can't seem to string two words together...

A beat while he struggles.

JAKE. She came back.

EDWARD. She came back. She was late. I'd put Leo to bed.
And... I just had this feeling. She kept denying it and
denying it, like I was mad.

Beat.

RACHEL. But finally she did.

JAKE (*sharply*). Just let him speak.

EDWARD. Yeah in the end she did.

Beat.

JAKE. And then what happened.

RACHEL (*sharply*). Stop *leading* him.

EDWARD. She said she's been having an affair with him for
the last two months.
    Apparently it started after Christmas.
    Apparently he asked her round to check out his poltergeist.
    Again.

RACHEL. God.

EDWARD. Opportunist prick. Using his poltergeist as a *wingman*.

JAKE. But *why*?

RACHEL. *Why* did she? Why *Tim*?

EDWARD *heaves a sigh*.

EDWARD. She said she wanted to make me see how it felt...
    when I cheated on her...

RACHEL. Yes...?

EDWARD. But then she *fell* for him.

RACHEL. She fell for Tim?

EDWARD. Tim, yes Tim! She's fallen for fucking Tim, I know!
    She's in love with him. The fucking hamster. They're 'in love'.

JAKE. ...But she's not going to *leave* you for him, is she?

EDWARD. She said she needed space to think... I said space to
    think where... She said Tim's... and then –

JAKE. Then?

EDWARD. ...I lost it. I thought I was going to be sick.
    I cried.
    We said a lot more things...
    We had sex.
    Then she left.

RACHEL. ...You had *sex*?

EDWARD. I didn't... I couldn't bear the idea that she was
    leaving me.

JAKE. Right.

Pause.

Well, that's a good sign. That you had sex. Potentially.

RACHEL. Is it?

JAKE. Yes. Ed. This will blow over. Take it from me. Look at
    me and Rachel.

EDWARD (*dully*). Kitty and I are nothing like you and Rachel.

JAKE. Yes, you are. (*To* RACHEL.) You felt I didn't
    understand, and –

RACHEL. You have no idea what I felt.

JAKE. Oh, fuck off. You said you felt I had no idea how you
    felt. Endlessly. So – I *do* know how you felt. And *you* did
    exactly the same thing as Kitty.

RACHEL. I did not.

JAKE. You gave Alan a blowjob. To teach me a lesson.

    Beat.

RACHEL. I did give Alan a blowjob, that is true.

JAKE (*impatiently*). – Like Kitty shagging Tim, to get your
    own back. It's nothing to be ashamed of. It focused me. And
    I took it like a man. Even though I hear it from *Jimmy*, mind.
    (*To* EDWARD.) Who walked in on them.
    'I came into the kitchen and Mummy was drinking a man's
    willy.'

RACHEL. Anyway. The point is. Anyway.

JAKE. We survived.

RACHEL. It's true.

JAKE. In fact, it *healed* us. It sort of felt fair. An eye for an eye,
    a tooth for a tooth.
    You can forgive. When you know Alan's cock has been
    sucked.

    EDWARD's *crying has become loudly audible once more
    and they are distracted.*

RACHEL (*in an undertone*). Oh God… is he *okay*…?

JAKE (*in an undertone*). Don't talk about him in the third
    person… he'll feel like he's going mad…

RACHEL (*in an undertone*). I've never *seen* him like this…

EDWARD (*overriding, obliviously*)....The crazy thing is, this
   is what Kitty *wanted*!! If she could see me now – she *wanted*
   me to be emotional. She *wanted* me to be jealous. I mean,
   I only had *sex* with her because I thought it was what she
   wanted. I thought I was showing *passion*.

JAKE....What... happened?

EDWARD. I told you.

   I can't put it into words. It's very hard to describe.
   She got violent.

   Beat.

JAKE. When?

EDWARD. After we'd had sex.

   Pause.

   She hit me in the face. She kicked me in the shins. She just
   went mental. She stabbed me in the arm with a fork.

JAKE. Jesus. *After* you'd had sex?

EDWARD. Yes.

RACHEL. What did *you* do?

EDWARD. Nothing. I tried to protect myself.

JAKE. But why...?

EDWARD. I said if she left me, I was going to take Leo.

   Beat.

   That was when she said, I raped her.

   Pause.

JAKE. Jesus Christ.

EDWARD. I know.

   Pause.

JAKE. *Had* you?

EDWARD. Of *course* not, Jake! What do you think I *am*? I'm worried about her mental health! She had post-natal depression after Leo –

RACHEL. *Did* she?

EDWARD. – People work themselves into a state where they *believe* stuff –

JAKE....But why that you *raped* her?

EDWARD. I don't know! Because she wants to hate me. Because she wants to justify taking Leo away from me.

Pause.

JAKE. When you were having sex, did she say no at any point?

EDWARD. It's all a bit of a blur.

JAKE. It's a simple question, Ed!

EDWARD....I suppose she *did* say no a couple of times. But I was saying no too. I was *crying*.
I was going 'Nooo, nooo.'
Oh God, take it from me, *it was not rape*! I'm not a violent man.

JAKE. They don't have to fight you off any more, you know that. All they have to do is say no.

RACHEL. Did you ask her consent?

EDWARD. Oh for God's sake, of course not! She's... my... we're...
It was... non-verbal.
It was *sex*.

JAKE. Rough sex?

Beat.

EDWARD. Didn't *you* want to have sex with Rachel when she said she was going to leave you?

JAKE. No. I wanted to *kill* her.
But I didn't. I controlled myself.

I actually broke this incisor, grinding my teeth trying *not* to hit her.

RACHEL (*to* EDWARD). You know what he did instead? He stamped on my foot. I was like, what are you, a twelve-year-old girl? At least grab me by the *throat*.

EDWARD....I thought we were making love! Why is what *she* thinks the truth?

JAKE. Because that's the *law*! Let me sum up. You knew she didn't want to. She said she was leaving you. She said she was in love with Tim. And then you have sex with her. Without her consent. It's a classic case of marital rape.

Pause.

EDWARD. In that case...

Beat.

In that case, I suppose you could say, *technically*, I raped her.

JAKE. Well – technically's what counts, isn't it, Ed?!

EDWARD. I wanted her to see I *cared*!

JAKE. So you fucked her? Bollocks! You were rubbing him out. With your dick.
It's not Kitty you're angry with, it's Tim.

RACHEL. Ed, this is crazy. You're rational. You're intelligent.

JAKE. If you're hurt enough, you become stupid.

RACHEL. Okay. You're a very intelligent, and in these particular circumstances, very... emotional person. Like *me*. I know exactly how you feel.

JAKE. Christ. Hell hath no fury like a man scorned, eh?

RACHEL. I've *been* there.

JAKE. Yeah. Thank God you haven't got a penis. Or you would have fucking raped *me*.

RACHEL. It's unbelievably painful when someone cheats on you. I know exactly how that feels, you're angry, can't think straight –

JAKE. That's not a reason to *rape* someone!

EDWARD. *I didn't rape her!* I *love* her.

JAKE. Yup, that's what a psychotic security guard says when he bludgeons his girlfriend to death with a claw hammer. Other end of the spectrum, Ed, same bullshit.

RACHEL (*with finality*). I'm on Ed's side.

JAKE. Well I'm not.

Pause.

EDWARD. Is she going to *use* it?

They think about this.

If she wants to get *technical*, by God I can get technical. The violence. The regular assaults.

JAKE. What *regular* assaults?

EDWARD. She hacked into my phone. That's a criminal act.

JAKE. You hacked into *hers*.

EDWARD. No. *Technically*, I didn't have to. There's no pin on her phone.

JAKE. For fuck's *sake*, Ed!

RACHEL. You're better than this.

EDWARD. The depression.

RACHEL. Kitty's not depressed.

EDWARD. *Yet.*

RACHEL. Ed!!

EDWARD. The fork – wounding me with intent. And she kicked me with her shod foot. A shod foot – that's classed as a weapon.

JAKE. Oh Ed, grow *up*!

EDWARD *starts to cry again.*

EDWARD. I don't know who she is any more.

I don't know who she is.

Scene Three

The same actress who played GAYLE, *who now speaks in RP, as* LAURA, *a solicitor, sits with* KITTY.

LAURA. It is best to put in an application *first*. Before the other party.

KITTY. He's threatened that he'd be asking for sole custody with me having visitation rights.

LAURA. We don't actually say custody any more. Because people fought over the badge, the title. Child arrangements order. Ghastly – anyway – on what grounds?

KITTY. Mental instability.

LAURA. Your...

KITTY. *My* mental instability.

LAURA *nods*.

My violence. My hormonal and emotional problems. He said he's putting together a sixty-page document about my depression.

LAURA. What is he alleging?

KITTY. Oh it's *laughable*. Things like when, Leo was a newborn, I left Leo in Sainsbury's at the deli counter and drove off. Without the baby.

LAURA *waits for more*.

I'd had no sleep! I'd *just* given birth! We *laughed* about it!!
It was funny!
It's ridiculous!

He talks about my inability to cope, that I was overwhelmed. I was *bored*! I wanted to go back to work! Who *doesn't* get depressed? I mean, it's *him* who's gone mad. That's the fucking thing!
I can't sleep. I'm on Temazepam. He can make the narrative plausible. It's terrifying. I mean, he's a barrister. It's what he does.

LAURA. Oh, he's a barrister?

KITTY. Yes.

EDWARD *appears, starts to talk to* LAURA, *who swivels on her wheelie chair to listen.*

EDWARD. Totally out of character. When she was conducting the affair she was going out at night to meet this man, using a babysitter who was not properly qualified. It's an unstable relationship with an unsettled future. She's putting her own interests ahead of the child's.

EDWARD/KITTY (*in unison*). I'm the better parent.

LAURA (*generally*). This sounds like classic narcissistic behaviour.

KITTY. I can't believe he's...
I'm not mad! – Can I smoke in here, it's only electric.
This all *started* because he didn't want me to *leave* him!
He said I'd have to divorce him before he'd leave the house.
It was him who brought up the *word*, divorce.
What I'm trying to say is that he's very very angry. He has a problem with anger.

LAURA. Right.

KITTY. We started to grow apart when – a complainant from one of his cases, an unstable woman who I think had almost certainly been raped, killed herself.

LAURA. Oh dear.

KITTY. She hung herself. He became very wrapped up in his work. That's when it all started to go wrong.

EDWARD. She never had boyfriends before me. She's
emotionally immature. She's convinced this relationship is
deep and lasting – it's not.

KITTY. I think you should know… that…
Before I left, he forced me to have sex with him.

EDWARD. The fact she claims this is a sign of her mental
instability.

LAURA. Right.

KITTY. He raped me.

LAURA. I see.

EDWARD/KITTY. Well?

Pause.

LAURA. Well I'm afraid it is quite hard to make it relevant to
the case. You see – that's not damaging to the *child*.
It's also irrelevant to the finances.

KITTY. Doesn't rape –

LAURA. Not really. It's violence against you, not the child.
It's the same with pornography, prostitutes – even in the
marital bed – not regarded as damaging to the child.
(*Brightening slightly.*) Unless it's *child* porn.

KITTY. So it wouldn't help my case?

LAURA. The view is, the violence is not going to be continued
because you will have separated. If you liked, you could press
criminal charges. Take it to a criminal court. You might well
have a case. But it does have a rather unfortunate air of tit for
tat. There is also the question of why you didn't report it at the
time. Rape comes under conduct and personally I avoid
conduct like the plague.

(*Generally.*) I wouldn't bother.

KITTY. Jesus Christ.

For a moment LAURA *drops her professional manner
a little.*

LAURA. The divorce system doesn't give much of a feeling of justice being done.
That's why people take justice into their own hands.

(*To* EDWARD.) Believe it or not, I am on your side. (*To* KITTY.) I went into divorce law when my marriage ended. My divorce was becoming a full-time job, I thought, why not make *divorce* my full-time job?

KITTY. What did you do before?

LAURA. Crime.

Scene Four

EDWARD, JAKE *and* RACHEL *sit in* JAKE *and* RACHEL'*s kitchen.* KITTY *stands apart.*

RACHEL. This is insanity. As soon as you go to court it just escalates things. It just ramps up the conflict. It's a crystallisation of the fact you loathe each other, which you don't.

JAKE. And it'll cost a fucking fortune.

RACHEL (*beseechingly*). Kitty.

JAKE. It'll be the end of his career. He'll have a criminal record. Even if he were acquitted his career would be fucked.

RACHEL (*to* EDWARD). Why are you *doing* this?

EDWARD (*indicating* KITTY). Ask her.

RACHEL. You're our friends. I can't bear to see you do this to each other.

EDWARD. Let her fucking speak!

Beat.

KITTY (*to* EDWARD). The reason I'm fighting you for Leo is that *you're* fighting me for Leo.

EDWARD. No. Let's get this straight. You're saying I *raped* you.

JAKE. If she's just doing it because you're taking *her* to court then it's very simple. Don't take her to court, for fuck's sake!

EDWARD (*to* JAKE *and* RACHEL). I can't recognise her. I can't recognise the woman who's doing this to me. (*To* KITTY.) I did not rape you. You *know* that's not the truth.

KITTY. It's *my* truth!

EDWARD. It's *not* the truth.

JAKE. Look. There's a world in which you're *both* telling the truth. But that's not the *law*. In court, your narratives are oil and water. They can never mix. One of you will win. And one of you will *lose*. Do you really want that? Do you really, really want that?

EDWARD. Yes.

JAKE. Ed. Seriously. Apart from anything, I think she's got a case.

EDWARD. I don't care if I lose, I want to *fight* her!

RACHEL. I thought you didn't *want* to go to court?

EDWARD. I changed my fucking mind. You fuck another man and then you take my kid? *He* gets my kid?? Fuck *off*! (*To* KITTY.) You *let* me have sex with you so you'd have it as a weapon. It's a *weapon*!

KITTY. Oh what, I'm hitting you in the face with your own *cock*?

RACHEL. Look, look, look. Stop. The thing none of us is asking, is was it *actually* a rape?

KITTY. *What??*

JAKE. By your own admission she said no, you went ahead, and therefore, I'm afraid, it was.

EDWARD. Yes but *when* did she think it was? When she needed a weapon! *Afterwards!*

RACHEL. I think Ed's got a point.

KITTY (*to* RACHEL). I'm sorry, *what* did you say?

RACHEL. Well, we don't know what actually happened, do we?

KITTY. I don't have to talk about this!

RACHEL. You're going to *have* to talk about it if you go through with it.

EDWARD. You may as well practise.

KITTY. Fuck you! Fuck *you*. He said he felt sick. I was crying.

EDWARD. We were both crying.

RACHEL. Ed, shut *up*.

KITTY. We hugged each other. He started to take off my clothes. I said no.

EDWARD. I was saying *sorry*.

KITTY. No, you said I *apologise*.

EDWARD. Jesus!!

KITTY. He took off all my clothes. He had sex with me.

EDWARD. And you had sex with me!

KITTY. I said 'no', several times.

EDWARD. And so did I!!

RACHEL. Where?

EDWARD. In the kitchen. On the floor.

KITTY. It was over quite quickly.

EDWARD. Because I couldn't maintain an erection!

KITTY. Then afterwards I got up and put my clothes on again. I said I was leaving. He said if I left he'd keep Leo.

EDWARD. Then you stabbed me in the arm with a fork and said I'd raped you.

KITTY. Right. So what did *you* think it was?

EDWARD. Actually? I thought it was a mercy fuck. I thought you were taking pity on me. That's what people *do*.

KITTY (*to* RACHEL). Well?

RACHEL. As far as I'm concerned calling that rape bankrupts the term rape.

JAKE (*to* RACHEL). As far as I'm concerned what *you've* just said bankrupts the term rape.

KITTY (*to* RACHEL). How *dare* you? You weren't there!

EDWARD. Don't tell me that I brutally raped you. It wasn't rape until you *needed* it to be rape.

KITTY (*to* RACHEL). Don't you always say there can't be *degrees* of rape? (*To* EDWARD.) I 'made' you rape me?? *I* premeditated your rape? Jesus, Ed. I'm not scarred. I'm not traumatised. No I didn't fight you off. You were *pathetic*. I actually felt *sorry* for you. But technically, you raped me!

RACHEL. Kitty, this is – that's not fair.

EDWARD. Okay, okay, okay. You want to talk about things we've done? When the other one said no? Four months ago, you had an abortion. You did what you wanted to do when *I* said no. I said no but you went ahead and did it.

KITTY. It's my body and I can do what I want with it.

EDWARD. It was *our* baby!

KITTY's phone rings. EDWARD snatches it off her.

KITTY. Give it – back – !!

EDWARD (*down the phone*). And *you* can fuck off, you fucking *hamster*!

He throws the phone down.

If you say I raped you, I'll say you're *mad*. Because you *are*.

KITTY. If you say I'm mad I'll say *you're* mad. Because you *are* fucking mad.

JAKE. Guys – you're *both* mad. And I've got fucking tinnitus.

EDWARD. Did she tell you? Did she tell you that, that she had an abortion? When she knew I was desperate for another child? (*To* KITTY.) You already *took* your revenge!

KITTY (*to* JAKE *and* RACHEL). He can't see how manipulative, how controlling he's being!

EDWARD. Am I the only one aware of the ironies here?!

KITTY (*to* EDWARD). You're using *Leo* as a weapon! You know that Leo is the way to hurt me and that's why you're trying to limit my access!

EDWARD. You're trying to limit *mine*! Taking Leo away from me, *that's* rape!

KITTY. Don't get *metaphorical* with me –

JAKE. Guys! You can go back and forth like this ad infinitum. You have to just / draw a line –

EDWARD. / If you say we should just draw a line, I'll fucking hit you. (*To* KITTY.) You took him away with you four weeks ago and I haven't seen him since. Don't talk to me about limiting fucking access.

Beat.

RACHEL. Kitty. Is that true?

KITTY. Do you blame me? After what he did?

The bell rings. RACHEL *goes to answer it.*

EDWARD. There's nothing more dangerous than self-righteousness, Kit.

KITTY. That is a bloody self-righteous thing to say.

EDWARD. I've said sorry and sorry and sorry. It'll *never* be enough for you. For someone who thinks the law is unfair, you're fucking *punitive*. Not being able to forgive is every bit as bad as not being able to say sorry. In fact, it *is* not being able to say sorry!

KITTY. Yes, that's right, *intellectual* origami –

EDWARD. I'm not being *intellectual origami*! Can't you see I'm hurting, you hurt me. Now I know how you felt. Satisfied? You got what you wanted, didn't you?

KITTY. Okay, yes. And it went somewhere else. I fell in love. (*To* JAKE.) Now I know what it's like being *you*. It's a fucking nightmare. It's a fucking mess, I made a fucking mess.

TIM *comes in*.

EDWARD. Oh God, it's the hamster.

TIM (*to* KITTY). Are you okay?

KITTY. Yes I'm okay.

EDWARD. Fuck *off*, you fucking hamster.

KITTY. Stop calling him that!

TIM. I was worried –

EDWARD. Sweetheart. (*To* KITTY.) He's a fucking poof.

TIM. I want to stay out of this –

EDWARD. Then fucking go away, *stay* out of it!

JAKE. Tim, I hate to interrupt – but did you pay for parking?

RACHEL. I gave him one of those tickets –

EDWARD (*laughing incredulously*). Jesus!

JAKE (*to* EDWARD). There's no reason for him to get a fine on top of everything else.

TIM. I'm not staying, anyway. Come on, Kitty.

KITTY. I'm coming. I don't know why I came.

EDWARD (*to* KITTY). We laughed about his BO together! I don't believe this! How did this *happen*? Christ, Kitty. You know who you remind me of? *Jake*. Next you'll be telling me when you make love, you '*make* love'. Look where your *empathy's* landed you. In the pond with fucking Jake.

JAKE (*pained*). Guys, I'd really appreciate it if you didn't keep using me as some kind of adultery *yardstick* – 'Jake: The Measure of a Turd' –

EDWARD (*ignoring him, to* TIM). So I cheated on her! Once. Years ago. You know that's *why* she fucked you? To get her own back on me. How does it feel? Being used?

TIM. Pretty good, actually.

KITTY. Oh God, let's fucking go.

EDWARD (*to* KITTY). You think you're getting your revenge – you're getting *his*! I can't believe he's got you doing it *for* him! He's *always* resented me. (*To* TIM.) Thou shalt not covet thy neighbour's wife –

TIM. You know, mate, you sound *desperate*. We're going.

EDWARD. How do you think Zara feels about all this, eh? Think about *her*, for a second? Where does *she* fit into all this?

TIM. None of your fucking business.

EDWARD *bars their way.*

EDWARD (*to* KITTY). It's just about winning. I know him. The minute he's won he'll lose interest. (*To* TIM.) She still cares about me or she wouldn't be punishing me. Revenge comes from a hot place, not a cold.

TIM. Which is why revenge is a dish best *eaten* cold.

EDWARD. She won't give you a child, you fuck.

TIM. How do you know? –

EDWARD. If she does I'll fucking kill it!

He rushes at TIM, *attempts to punch him,* JAKE *pulls him off.*

JAKE. Jesus, Ed! Stop it! Guys. Please. What *is* this!

EDWARD *stands, breathing heavily,* TIM *straightens his shirt.*

KITTY (*generally*). You see what I'm dealing with? *Leo* has more self-control!

TIM (*to* EDWARD). Fuck you –

JAKE. Actually, mate, I think it would be better if you *did* stay out of this. Just for the moment.

TIM *takes a few steps back*.

EDWARD (*to* KITTY). Why? Why are you doing this?

Beat.

I love you.

KITTY (*to* EDWARD). I'm in love with him.

EDWARD. Fine. You want a fight – I'll fight.

Scene Five

ZARA *stands in* KITTY *and* EDWARD'*s kitchen. The atmosphere is still*.

ZARA *is dressed all in black. A pause*.

KITTY. Look, I am.

I'm really sorry.

Beat.

Ed and I have been… for years… I know it sounds mad but I had to make him see.

ZARA *is looking at* KITTY.

ZARA. What's wrong with your *face*?

Beat.

KITTY. I've just come back from the dentist's…

She massages her face, winces.

Had a… had to have a filling…

Pause.

ZARA. You felt he'd never know what it was like to be cheated on until you did it to him.

KITTY. Yes.

ZARA. You were punishing him.

KITTY. I suppose.

ZARA. You could have just slept with Tim, then that would have been that? Tit for tat?

KITTY *feels her numb mouth.*

KITTY. Yes.

ZARA. You thought you were going to be very *judicious*, mete out a bit of retribution and be very *fair*.

KITTY. I had no idea I was going to feel the way I felt once I'd done it.

ZARA. No. You might have thought about that first.

So what was *I*? Your collateral?

KITTY. I promise you, it wasn't about you.

ZARA. Yeah, not for *you* it wasn't. It was for *me*. For *me* it was about me.

Not very *fair*.

KITTY. I didn't realise – you can't legislate for – for human behaviour.

ZARA. I thought that was exactly what you were *doing*?

KITTY. I mean you can't help your feelings. You can't help how you feel.

ZARA. You? Or do you mean *me*?

KITTY. ...Both of us.

She massages her cheek.

(So numb... itchy.)

ZARA. Yes you can.

You've got everything. The house, the child, the husband.
Why *him*, as well? You're fucking *greedy*.

Beat.

You aren't happy. Yeah I remember hearing all about that.
How you didn't want *another*.

For me this is about a baby. It's about a child.

I don't buy it, actually. Isn't it more that it's annoying, when
someone who's *always* fancied you finds someone else at
last... and your sex life with Ed was... well, you told me,
how *boring* it was... sitting on his face for the umpteenth
time... but all that doesn't fit with your *idea* of yourself,
does it? Sounds sort of petty, doesn't it?

We were trying for a baby.

KITTY. Yes.

Beat.

I feel terrible.

ZARA. What do you *mean*, terrible? You don't feel terrible, you
feel guilty.

KITTY. Yes.

ZARA. What's feeling guilty? Feeling sorry? Sorry for *yourself*.
But not sorry enough to stop.

ZARA looks around.

KITTY. He's still in his place.

ZARA. Who is?

KITTY. He is. Tim.

ZARA. I wasn't asking.
So now you've got *two* houses.

KITTY.... We're selling it. This one.

Beat.

ZARA. I was just wondering where's your kid? With the nanny?

The thing I don't understand is, why make all that fuss when you pay for someone to take him off you anyway?

Beat. She starts to cry.

What the fuck am I meant to do now? Start again? Find someone else?

KITTY. I don't know.

ZARA. You've already *got* one. You *twat*.
Empathy. You think you're so empathetic. You're fucking *ruthless*.

Who are you to dole out judgement? I'm sure it was very restorative for *you*.

You know you drive every man you're with *mad*. Ed. Tim.

Ed's in a *real* state.

KITTY. I'm sorry.

ZARA. Stop saying sorry, you keep saying sorry, stop saying sorry and be a nicer fucking person.

KITTY. I dropped the charges.

A beat in which ZARA *gathers herself.*

ZARA. Ed rang me up. We had a long chat.

I told him all the things you told me. What you said about his *penis* size.
The pass your *boss* made at you.
How you ended up snogging that Australian in the car park at the wedding.

KITTY. Okay. Good.

ZARA. *All* that stuff we chatted about. I thought it was relevant.

KITTY. Yes.

Pause.

I'm sor–

ZARA. Oh shut up, will you? An apology has to *cost* something or it isn't an apology. If it doesn't make you sorry, you're not sorry. That's why we punish people – to make them feel sorry. According to you, right? You force them, literally, to empathise with you. You're unhappy so you make them unhappy. You were unhappy so you made Ed unhappy.

KITTY *nods, slowly.*

EDWARD *in* TIM*'s house. He looks around.*

EDWARD. Big.

TIM. Yeah.

Beat.

EDWARD. Yeah, yep.

It would just really help me to know why.

TIM. I don't know why.

EDWARD *looks around the room.*

EDWARD. You're letting yourself off the hook.

TIM (*shaking his head*). When you boil an egg the structure of the molecules change. The egg doesn't know why. It just becomes a boiled egg. I'm not justifying myself.

EDWARD. That is exactly what you're doing. Every time you speak you justify yourself.

What's the voice in your head? At the supermarket?

TIM. I don't have one.

EDWARD. What about all the arrangements? The *logistics* of it? The texting, the *timetabling*? You're telling me your mind was a *blank*? During all that? It takes a lot of *organisation*. I *know*. What were you *thinking*?

TIM. I wasn't thinking anything. There was no narrative. She was the one cheating on you. Not me.

EDWARD. You were cheating on me. On our friendship.

TIM. We're not friends. You hate me and I hate you. Slightly more.

Morality's not innate. It's learnt. We only feel shame when we're witnessed.
And sometimes not even then.

EDWARD. But we witness ourselves.

Beat. EDWARD *sits down.*

Jake's kid has just started getting interested in dragons.
That's what he's drawing now. And knights.
When I was at school I got into trouble for pulling down the Christmas decorations in the classroom. The paper chains.
I got carried away with the feeling.

Back to KITTY *and* ZARA.

ZARA. Ed's going to help me out.

This is what I need. I'm running out of time. I can't fuck about.

KITTY *winces, puts her hand into her mouth, feels something.*

You don't want another, do you? And you don't want *him* any more. He's doing a good thing. Don't worry, I don't fancy him.

KITTY *takes out a cotton stick. It is drenched and bloody.*

It's *fair*, isn't it?

Pause. KITTY *looks at the stick.*

KITTY. Yes. I suppose it is fair.

ZARA *looks, off.*

ZARA. He said it would be here.

She walks offstage.

Back to EDWARD *and* TIM. EDWARD *gets up, comes closer to* TIM.

EDWARD. What's that smell?

TIM. What smell?

Pause.

EDWARD. It's aftershave. Your aftershave.

TIM. Yeah.
Kitty gave it to me.

EDWARD. It's the same as mine.

You smell like me.

He leaves. TIM *looks after him.*

KITTY *waits for* ZARA *to return.*

ZARA *talks from off. Rattling noises.*

ZARA. God you've got a lot of crap in here… you need to
spring clean…

Ah.

She comes back in with the counterweight.

Ed said he wants it for his flat.

They stare at each other.

Scene Six

KITTY *and* EDWARD*'s house. Some time later. Late-afternoon light. There is a dust sheet over the sofa. Some cardboard boxes. A bit like the first scene.* EDWARD *stands,* KITTY *is sitting on the sofa. Very bleak.*

Silence.

EDWARD. We never did decide where to put it.

Do you want it?

KITTY. No.

Pause.

EDWARD. Can't *believe* how expensive cardboard boxes are... I thought they were free.

KITTY. Yeah.

EDWARD *plucks at the sheet on the sofa.*

Kristoff didn't want to get paint on it.

EDWARD. Oh right.

Well, he's done a great job.

Pause.

Funny light at this time of day, isn't it?

KITTY *looks up at the ceiling.*

KITTY. The bulb must have gone.

EDWARD. When are the viewings?

KITTY. Next week.

EDWARD. Well. We may as well take this off then.

KITTY *wearily gets up off the sofa.* EDWARD *pulls the sheet off the sofa. It has marks of paint and stains on it. He billows it out, waiting for* KITTY *to take the other end.*

KITTY. Why?

Beat.

We're just going to throw it, anyway.

EDWARD *billows it out again. Reluctantly, slowly,* KITTY *takes the other end of the marked and spotted sheet. Slowly, they start to fold.*

EDWARD. No wait... it's not quite... put the edges...

He matches his corners more carefully to KITTY*'s.*

KITTY.... What does it matter...?

EDWARD. Half again...

They carry on folding. Slowly. Silently. Each fold brings them closer to one another.

...I heard about Tim. Going back. To Zara.

KITTY. Yeah.

EDWARD. Well.

KITTY. Yeah.

EDWARD. I was sorry.

KITTY. Don't talk crap.

EDWARD. At least she'll get her baby now. God knows what it'll *look* like, but.
Smell like... BO probably...

I felt sorry for you.

KITTY. No you didn't.

EDWARD. Yes, I did. I was sorry for *you*. I can't forgive *him*. He came in, fucked us up and then left again.

Pause.

But I do know what you must feel like.

I know what it feels like now.

I know how much it hurts.

Pause. KITTY *looks at him.*

KITTY. Really.

EDWARD. Yes.
What you did worked.

Pause. The dirty sheet is now neatly folded.

Hey.

KITTY *looks at him.*

We did well.

KITTY. What do you mean?

EDWARD. We did well. Even to achieve this.

Pause.

KITTY. I don't know what you mean.

KITTY *puts the sheet into* EDWARD*'s hands.*

Pause.

EDWARD. I'm sorry.

KITTY. What?

EDWARD. I said, I'm sorry.

KITTY *doesn't say anything.*

I'm sorry.

EDWARD *gets down on his knees.*

KITTY. What are you *doing*?

EDWARD. I'm saying sorry. Forgive me.

KITTY. Oh get *up*.

EDWARD. Please.

KITTY. Get up, for God's sake, get up.

EDWARD. Please. Forgive me.

KITTY. Stop it. Please.

EDWARD. Why.

KITTY. Because.

EDWARD. Why?

KITTY *is getting tearful.*

KITTY. Because you're making me feel sorry for you.

EDWARD. Forgive me. Fucking forgive me.

KITTY *tries to pull him up. It doesn't work. Slowly she gets down and kneels in front of him. Their hands are on each other's shoulders – half-grapple, half-embrace. Silently, GAYLE's ghost appears at the back of the room, where she stood at the start of the play. She watches them.*

Fade to black.

www.nickhernbooks.co.uk

 facebook.com/nickhernbooks

 twitter.com/nickhernbooks